Alternatives
to
American
Mainline
Churches

Joseph H. Fichter
Editor

Conference series no. 14
First edition
© 1983
Unification Theological Seminary
Barrytown, New York 12507

Printed in the United States of America
Library of Congress Catalog Number 82-50819
ISBN 0-932894-14-3

Distributed by
The Rose of Sharon Press, Inc.
G.P.O. Box 2432
New York, New York 10116

CONTENTS

Introduction: Choice of Alternatives

Joseph H. Fichter

The three main categories of organized religion in America are commonly labeled Protestant, Catholic and Jewish even though everyone knows that some religious groups cannot be subsumed within any of these three. It is also clear that none of these is an undifferentiated organization, which means that members in each of them already have alternative choices of affiliation. Jews may identify with Orthodox, Conservative or Reform branches of their religion; the number of alternative denominations within Protestantism offers a great variety of prospective affiliations; and the manifestations of American Catholicism tend to reflect different ethnic backgrounds and class status.

The purpose of this book is to look outside of this well-known Protestant-Catholic-Jew religious "catchall" and to investigate a few examples of fringe groups, organizations that are different from conventional American religions. Some of them can be termed "new" only because they have been newly and recently introduced to this country—mainly from Asian sources. In some ways they may be a demonstration of the so-called new religious "consciousness" that is said to pervade the youth of America.[1] In other words, Americans have an increasing number of alternatives from which to choose when they want to activate this religious consciousness. They also have more substitutes for religion, groups like the Human Potential Movement, Transcendental Meditation, Spiritualism and various cultural programs for self-actualization. Many of these may be included in the so-called metaphysical movement in which behavioral commitments tend to avoid theological principles.

The conference at which these papers were read and discussed was ecumenical in the varying religious affiliations of the participants as well as in its sponsorship by the New Ecumenical Research Association, known also as New ERA.

The three-day meeting was hosted by the Institute of Pastoral Studies on the Chicago campus of Loyola University. Dr. J. Gordon Melton, director of the Institute for the Study of American Religion, facilitated the conference and moderated its sessions. Scholars from the United States, Canada and Great Britain were invited to contribute papers on alternative American religions.

Discussions at the conference ranged from psychological interpretations of religious movements to methodological proposals for research analysis. The papers that were selected and edited for this volume reflect historical and sociological perspectives. They do not focus on the "newness" or foreign origin of these alternative religious groups, but on the fact that they are *different* from conventional American churches and denominations. The case studies that emerge from the Chicago conference can be divided into a category of metaphysical movements and another of religious movements.

Conceptualizations

The need to separate genuine religions from their secular imitations is met by the definitional clarifications of the first two chapters of this book. The ordinary citizen has no difficulty in accepting the notion that religion involves a "belief in Spiritual Beings," and that people who affiliate themselves with religious groups do profess some form of relationship with a divinity. A church differs functionally from a school, or a factory, or an athletic club, and most people are clearly willing to make such distinctions. Most sociologists of religion too identify organized religion as a group of believers whose symbols and activities focus on the "beyond."[2] As Stark and Bainbridge point out, the essential element in the search for ultimate meaning among religious devotees is the postulate that supernatural being, or force, or power, is ready to influence actively human events and conditions here on earth.[3]

While there are many and confusing definitions of

religion, and while the major elements of these definitions have been debated at great length,[4] there should be no real problem in separating religion from non-religion; that is, to recognize genuine alternative forms of religion on the one hand, and *ersatz* alternatives to religion on the other. This is not a question of the truth of any set of basic theological beliefs and religious practices. Certainly the scientific methods of empirical research are not competent to allow sociologists to discern whether Lutherans have a "truer" religion than Baptists, or Jews than Christians. Nevertheless, from a functional perspective it ought to be easily possible to distinguish a religious organization from a secular organization. Even the American courts—for legal and fiscal reasons—have occasionally been called upon to define an organized religion. The establishment of religion and the exercise thereof have been sensitive areas of legal contention, highlighted recently by "conservatorship orders" allowing parents to interfere with the religious affiliation of their adult children.[5]

Belief or unbelief in a deity serves as a useful criterion to distinguish between metaphysical movements and religious movements. It is useful also to distinguish between metaphysics, as a division of Aristotelean philosophy and the concept of metaphysics that "stands for the deeper realities of the universe,"[6] the things which are external— which stand above and beyond the outer phenomenal realm. It is much more difficult to reach agreement on a set of criteria for the construction of a typology in which all of these groups and movements may be contained. From a sociological perspective, social relations, roles and structures may not differ greatly between genuine and substitute religions. A religious movement like the electronic churches may be as unstructured as a metaphysical movement like the Spiritual Frontiers Fellowship. Both the Society of Krisha Consciousness and the Secret Order of Thelemic Magick are hierarchical, but one is a religion and the other is not.

Arguments about the building of religious categories

and the ordering of typologies generally take their rise in the church-sect dichotomy introduced by Max Weber and subsequently expanded by Ernst Troeltsch and others.[7] The notion that the presence or absence of tension between the group and its society can be the criterion for measuring the difference between church and sect, is disputed by Professor David Martin. The Anglican, Catholic and Presbyterian churches are in tension at the present time in Northern Ireland, but they do not cease to be churches. There was a time when the Catholic Church cooperated harmoniously with political regimes in South America—and thus fit the definition of *ecclesia.* The contemporary and growing tension with some of the Latin American governments, however, does not reduce that church definitionally to a religious sect or cult.

The single criterion of social tension suggests that sects and cults tend to be in varying degrees of conflict with the surrounding sociocultural environment. One reason for the tension is that the cult considers the larger society secular and sinful, but the outside observer may note also that the cult is at odds with the larger society because it is novel, or foreign, or exotic, and thus the object of suspicion and distrust. Professor Martin prefers to focus on the individualism of cult members who belong to what he calls a "self" religion. They are less interested in worshipping together and in criticizing the larger society than they are in obtaining personal grace and individual benefits. From this point of view they may be classified under the heading the "client cult," as described by Stark and Bainbridge.

There are many other strands of argument, and the theoretical issues of conceptualization are still open to the divergent views presented in the first two chapters of this book. Even the notion that a person must choose a single group for exclusive membership is open to question when we learn that Scientologists may have dual membership, devotees of the Spiritual Frontiers Fellowship are encouraged to attend their original churches, and even the Moonies have no inhibitions about participating in the religious services of other churches.

Since all of the groups described in these case studies are alternatives to the conventional American religions they may share the label of cultural deviants. The International Society for Krishna Consciousness is deviant as a cultural importation, while the Spiritual Frontiers Fellowship deviates as a cultural innovation. Another type of deviance is apparent in the sectarian tendencies of the Catholic Traditionalist Movement, which is not a sect, and the leaders of which insist that the parent body even in its Vatican representatives has strayed from orthodoxy. The case of the electronic churches represents another kind of deviance which may move in the direction of an ecclesiastical coalition, an array of Protestant denominations, or simply a series of branch outlets of existing American churches.

Every academic conference, as well as the publication that emerges from it, pretends to subscribe to some unifying theme, no matter how vague and abstruse. Even when we are looking at alternatives to American religion, and even when the authors carefully define each movement as different from other movements, we may still suggest that a common characteristic of the members of all the different groups is the "search for meaning." Even when the search leads to an answer in a this-worldly philosophy, as in Scientology, or in some spirit-world, as in Thelemic Magick and the Spiritual Frontiers Fellowship, the pursuit may be as authentic as the other-worldly religious search for "ultimate" meaning. At different levels and with varying preconceptions, the seekers who are described in this book are bound with a thin thread of similarity in the object of their search.

Metaphysical Alternatives

The general category of organizations that are identified as affiliates of the American metaphysical movements subscribe to a practical (and natural) philosophy of religion which focuses on the spiritual growth of the individual rather than on the praise and worship of God.[8] The so-called "transcendental theology" that underlies, and gave birth to, the metaphysical movement is attributed to a famous sermon by William E. Channing in which he said "the divine attributes are first developed in ourselves, and thence transferred to our Creator. The idea of God, sublime and awful as it is, is the idea of our own spiritual nature, purified and enlarged to infinity."[9] This soon came to mean that personal religious experience must precede objective religious knowledge, but in large part the pragmatic result has been "self" religion, or a system of belief and behavior that begins and ends with the individual. It is for this reason that we classify as non-religious metaphysical movements the three sociocultural groupings: The Spiritual Frontiers Fellowship, the Order of Thelemic Magick, and Scientology.

When we say that metaphysical movements are substitutes for religion, we do not mean that the members of these groups are atheists. Many of them are probably pragmatists, sophists, nominalists, and a pale imitation of the young Harvard intellectuals who formed the "Metaphysical Club" in the 1860s. The Spiritual Frontiers Fellowship encourages its members to discover the "inner God," that is, the divinity which is present in everyone. There is a deliberate and official avoidance of specific theological doctrines or fixed rituals. Whatever "works" for any individual is that in which faith must be placed. This metaphysical and personal experience seems reminiscent of Luckmann's theory of an "invisible religion" which limits transcendence to an existential area just above the human biological level of existence.[10] While the Fellowship helps people to respond to some of the psychic and spiritual needs ordinarily satisfied by authentic religion, it remains still a substitute for conventional religion.

The local unit of the Spiritual Frontiers Fellowship is

the Study Group which disbands when its scheduled class program is complete. The devotees maintain their membership by continuing to pay dues to the national headquarters but this is not in compliance to authority. The spirit of individualism forestalls the development of a hierarchical structure. Dr. Wagner's study shows no apparent tension between the Fellowship and the sociocultural environment, either at the local or national level. The organization deliberately encourages its members to maintain affiliation with conventional churches and to bring their psychic practices with them. The Fellowship, therefore, is obviously not a sect that separated from a parent body. Another reason for lack of tension is that the cultural values and practices of the membership are generally in conformity with American individualism and secularism.

Even further removed from the category of authentic religion are the members of the *Ordo Templi Orientis* who focus on the peculiar and mystical rituals of thelemic magick. The spirit entities with whom they make contact are in no way similar to the angels and saints of the Judeo-Christian tradition. In some instances they anticipate the overthrow of Christianity by the connivance of *Beast 666*, interpreted from the Book of Revelation as the reincarnation of the tyrant Nero. Dr. Melton shows elsewhere—in his scholarly Encyclopedia—that the ''Magick Family'' includes occult practitioners of witchcraft, Neo-Paganism and Satanism.[11] Their rituals and incantations are intended not only to evoke ancient secret wisdom which predates Christianity, but also to open the way to a new Aeon, the post-Christian world of tomorrow.

This secret society of magicians is meant to operate through a strict hierarchy of degrees of membership, the lower subservient to the higher, even to the Caliph, Magus, or Outer Head. In fact, however, there is an almost constant realignment of authority and groups. The definition of cult as strange, foreign, exotic—and in this case even erotic—

fits the collectivity and brings it into disrepute with both religious leaders and civil authorities. The peculiar rituals of sexual magick make these people a special focus for popular curiosity. Otherwise, the group may be appraised as simply another example of the popular patterns of astrology, spiritualism, palm-reading and general occultism.

Besides the Spiritual Frontiers Fellowship and the Thelemic Magicians, we discuss here the Scientologists, who claim that they are guided by an applied religious philosophy, but seem to fit better the category of non-religious, psychic and metaphysical movements. Nevertheless, the American founder of this controversial organization, Ron Hubbard, had it officially declared the Church of Scientology so that he could gain entrance to hospitals, asylums and prisons for the practice of his esoteric psychic techniques.[12] Professor Flinn proposes the interesting thesis that the practicing member of Scientology resembles in some respects a "space-age" Buddhist. Throughout the system there is little attention to meditation or contemplation, and even less to a relationship with the deity. The focus of practice is mental therapy which evolved from the "scientific" research effort of the founder, and not from divine revelation. Critics claim that Scientology is mental therapy masquerading as religion.

If the degree of "tension" between an organization and its larger society is the criterion distinguishing *ecclesia* from cult, the Scientologists must be described as more cultlike than churchlike. It is the debatable thesis of Roy Wallis that Scientology evolved from a cultic movement to an authentic sect, although there is no traditional church or denomination from which it separated itself.[13] Lawsuits, press exposure, police raids, governmental hostility, and other forms of public antagonism, have tended to minimize Scientology's claims to spiritual respectability. In an analogous sense, however, the organization has some church-like characteristics in its rituals and beliefs, in the development of a kind of professional ministry who supervise entrance ceremonials for new members and officiate at marriages and funerals. While the primary purpose of the "auditing technology" is a mental cure that assures personal freedom and awareness, the members demonstrate concern for the solution of social problems. Many of them, however, also maintain their affiliation with some conventional American church, a clear indication that they do not consider Scientology a rival religious movement.

Religious Alternatives

While the several *metaphysical* movements we have discussed are at best analogous surrogates for genuine religions, the four case studies we introduce here are religious organizations alternative to the conventional churches on the American scene. Each of them professes belief in the living God, has a professional ministry and sacred scriptures, is formally structured and provides rituals, prayers and worship services. Two of them, however, are "alternatives," in the sense that they are not indigenous to the United States. The International Society for Krishna Consciousness, although incorporated in New York City, draws its religious tradition from India, while the Holy Spirit Association for the Unification of World Christianity, was founded in Korea by Sun Myung Moon. The electronic church is an American invention, providing a modern technological and different way of spreading the Christian gospel. Most members of the Catholic Traditionalist Movement are Americans, but its strongest charismatic and sacramental support comes from a dissident French Archbishop.

During the course of a year's research Professor Larry Shinn lived as a participating observer with Krishna devotees in their temples in India as well as in the United States. He was interested in the conversion process through which young Americans left their traditional western religions to become members of the International Society for Krishna Consciousness. While acknowledging the typical sociocultural and psychological factors of conversion, he recognized the deep spiritual or religious motivations that are often undervalued or even dismissed by secular scholars. The members make an institutional commitment, serve under a spiritual guru, are initiated into a lifelong religious profession, and in their prayer, mantra recitation, and contemplation seek a deep spiritual relationship with God.

The organized Krishna movement, as a product of Eastern mysticism, is typically viewed as countercultural in the United States.[14] The devotees are vegetarians who avoid addictions to drugs, alcohol and tobacco. They are withdrawn from the materialism and sensate secularism of the western urban culture, but are conspicuous with their shaven heads and saffron robes and their occasional public festivals. They have been prosecuted for peddling without a license, and their zealous solicitation for donations is largely responsible for airport announcements warning of their presence. The detailed case study of Rama Dasa's spiritual pilgrimage to God serves as a refutation of the charges that young Krishna members are systematically and unwittingly brainwashed.

A religious movement of a different kind is described by William Dinges in his analysis of Catholic Traditionalism. A social movement is usually defined as an organized effort to bring about some needed change in the social structure, but in some cases it is also a deliberate attempt to prevent change, to retain and support cultural values of the past.[15] The several segments of the Catholic Traditionalist Movement are united in their resistance to the so-called *aggiornamento*, the significant up-dating of Catholic beliefs and behavior introduced by the Second Vatican Council in the 1960s. The champion of this movement is a French Archbishop who has been in defiance of explicit papal directives but who continues to guide this far-flung organization even while under suspension of his canonical and sacerdotal powers.

The earliest expression of protest against the conciliar reforms was made in the United States even while the Council was still in progress. The core of this protest was the insistence that the Council of Trent (1545-1563) had permanently fixed the unique and immutable characteristics of Catholicism, and that any deviation from the Tridentine decrees must necessarily lead the church into heresy. It is more than accidental that Father Francis Fenton called his branch of the organization the *Orthodox* Roman Catholic Movement, and that the Traditionalists place their collective loyalty in the liturgical preservation of the Tridentine Mass as originally celebrated in the Latin tongue. Dr. Dinges makes a careful distinction between conservative Catholics who remain loyal to the hierarchy and Traditionalist Catholics who feel that the American hierarchy has ''sold out'' to the secularists and that the Vatican itself has been infiltrated by dangerous heretics.

The Traditionalist Movement presents an alternative option for the practice of the Catholic religion even though it exists under the shadow of heavy Vatican disapproval. The organization has an authentic ministry of approximately ninety American priests now being augmented by younger clergy who are validly (though illicitly) ordained by Archbishop Lefebvre. These priests celebrate the Tridentine Mass in more than two hundred places, give sermons and other doctrinal instructions, and provide the sacraments for their loyal following of lay Catholics. From a sociological perspective they appear to be on the verge of sectarianism and schism, but they are ideologically and deeply attached to what they perceive as the orthodox and unchangeable faith of the traditional Roman Catholic Church. Vatican officials are loathe to pronounce excommunication, and the Traditionalists themselves are insistent that the official church has slipped into error.

Professor Jeffrey Hadden analyzes a large structural variation that presents an alternative method for conventional western Christianity to reach the masses with the gospel of salvation. The television preachers, with one exception, are mainly representative of fundamentalist and conservative Protestant denominations. Their simple biblical faith is a repudiation of the liberal theology they see in the mainline Protestant churches, and especially in the doctrines of "secular humanism," which they condemn as a perversion of traditional Christianity. The televangelists are intent on restoring morality to the individual, the family and the total society.[16] For this reason they extend their preaching mission to include political lobbying in favor of legislative moral reform.

The religious alternative provided by the electronic churches is the opportunity for millions of Americans to hear the word of God in their own comfortable homes in place of the conventional worship services at a local church. This case study finds that the loss of communicants and their financial support is seen as a serious threat to the continued existence of stable congregations and denominations. A certain degree of tension has grown between the conventional churches and the electronic churches, not only because of this present competition, but also from the threat that faithful audiences of the televangelists may be drawn into separate congregations and even into new religions. To the extent that leaders and followers among the electronic churches identify themselves as the "moral majority" of the American population and as the arbiters of public and private morality, they seem to arouse an attitude of antagonism on the part of many secularized Americans.

The "electric" church, as Ben Armstrong calls it, is a religious movement unlike any of the other organizations discussed in this book. He thinks that the viewers who support the specific religious teleview programs should be recognized as members or parishioners affiliated with the particular televangelist. Jerry Falwell says just the opposite, probably to avoid criticism from the pastors of local congregations. He argues, as do the leaders of the Billy Graham

Evangelistic Association, that the television program is not an "alternative to the church"; it is not a "church unto itself" but a means of getting the unsaved to join a congregation.[17] The pastoral ministry of the local clergy, like home visitation, counselling, Bible study, Sunday school, youth activities, cannot be provided in the electronic Christian ministry. The functional core of the typical Protestant religious "fellowship" is obviously absent from the electronic churches.

The fourth case study of a religious movement presents an alternative "parochial system" devised by the Unification Church as a means of reaching non-members in the local neighborhood. From a sociological perspective, the home church is a substitute for the well-organized and typical congregation which tends to be exclusive of non-members. It is difficult to discover who "belongs" to the home church, even though Eileen Barker sees the participants as associate Moonies who accept the doctrines of *Divine Principle*, but "do not commit themselves to living in a centre or to working full time for the Unification Church."[18] The physical "territory" encompasses a circle of 360 families, or household units, the inhabitants of which may never have heard of the church but who are the objective of the pastoral ministrations of a full-time committed Moonie.

The program of the home church has its origins in the earlier experiences of dedicated members who spent forty days of personal service to people in some designated areas. It was collectively initiated in the summer of 1978 when Moonie missionaries from many countries converged on England. Up to that time the Unification Church was similar to a religious order whose members dedicated their whole lives to the work of the church as "professionals" but allowed no room for the ordinary laity who make up the bulk of membership in the typical religious movement. While the local leaders are for the most part still full-time members of the church, a change is gradually taking place so that these positions can be taken by blessed couples who have jobs and families and social ties which they intend to maintain even after conversion to the Unification Church.

The home church introduces a relatively novel approach to the practice of systematic religiosity. The primary purpose is not to gain converts but to serve the needs of the community in whatever way those needs are manifested. This offer of voluntary service is greeted with skepticism by Americans steeped in privacy and individualism. It is seen as strange and peculiar behavior even among Christians who know Jesus' clear teaching that the way to salvation lies in the service of one's fellow human beings. Ultimately people begin to ask why the Moonies are behaving in this way, and the opportunity arises for an explanation of *Divine Principle*.

NOTES

1 See the eclectic variety discussed in Charles Y. Glock and Robert N. Bellah, eds., *The New Religious Consciousness* (Berkeley: University of California Press, 1976).

2 See Thomas O'Dea, *The Sociology of Religion* (Englewood Cliffs, N.J.: Prentice-Hall, 1966), pp. 1-2.

3 See also Rodney Stark, "Must All Religions Be Supernatural?" in Bryan Wilson, ed., *The Social Impact of New Religious Movements* (Barrytown, N.Y.: Unification Theological Seminary, distr. Rose of Sharon Press, 1981), pp. 159-77.

4 On the problems of definition see J. Milton Yinger, *The Scientific Study of Religion* (New York: Macmillan, 1970), pp. 3-17.

5 See the section, "On the Civil Liberties of Sect Members," in Irving Louis Horowitz, ed., *Science, Sin, and Scholarship* (Cambridge: MIT Press, 1978), pp. 192-216.

6 See J. Stillson Judah, *The History and Philosophy of the Metaphysical Movements in America* (Philadelphia: Westminster Press, 1967), p. 11.

7 See the lively discussion of the church-sect distinction by H.J. Demerath III and Phillip Hammond, *Religion in Social Context: Tradition and Transition* (New York: Random House, 1969), pp. 69-77, 157-63.

8 Members of the "Metaphysical Family" include thirty-one New

Thought groups and five kinds of Christian Scientists. See J. Gordon Melton, *The Encyclopedia of American Religions* (Wilmington: McGrath, 1978), II: 59-81, who traces their origins to Phineas Quimby who was introduced to mesmerism and animal magnetism in 1838.

9 This discourse was preached at the ordination of Reverend F. A. Farley in 1828. See Joseph Blau, ed., *American Philosophic Addresses, 1700-1900* (New York: Columbia University Press, 1946).

10 "We said that the organism transcends its biological nature by developing a Self and felt justified in calling that process fundamentally religious." Thomas Luckmann, *The Invisible Religion* (New York: Macmillan, 1967), p. 50. See also remarks of J. Stillson Judah, pp. 86-91.

11 J. Gordon Melton, "The Magick Family," in *Encyclopedia of American Religions*, chap. 18, pp. 249-305. Aleister Crowley is called "The Beast Himself," in Colin Wilson, *The Occult* (New York: Random House, 1971), pp. 349-75.

12 Omar V. Garrison, *The Hidden Story of Scientology* (Secaucus, N.J.:Citadel Press, 1974).

13 Roy Wallis, *The Road to Total Freedom: A Sociological Analysis of Scientology* (New York: Columbia University Press, 1977).

14 See J. Stillson Judah, *Hare Krishna and the Counter-culture* (New York: Wiley & Sons, 1974).

15 Lewis M. Killian, "Social Movements: A Review of the Field," in Robert R. Evans, ed., *Social Movements: A Reader and Source Book* (Chicago: Rand McNally, 1973).

16 The content of their theology is in Jeffrey Hadden and Charles Swann, "The Sermon from the Satellite," in *Prime Time Preachers* (Reading: Addison-Wesley, 1981), pp. 85-102.

17 *Ibid.*, pp. 178-79.

18 See Eileen Barker, "Who'd Be A Moonie?" in Bryan Wilson, ed., *The Social Impact of New Religious Movements* (Barrytown, N.Y.: Unification Theological Seminary, distr. Rose of Sharon Press, 1981), pp. 59-96.

Part I: Conceptualizations

Concepts for a Theory of Religious Movements

Rodney Stark and William Sims Bainbridge

Conceptual schemes abound in the scientific study of religion.[1] Definitions of major concepts have been amended, reconceived, and disputed at length. Most scholars limit religion to systems of thought and activity predicated on the existence of the supernatural,[2] but an articulate minority demands a definition of religion be broad enough to include scientific humanism, Marxism, and other non-supernatural philosophies.[3] This is a critical dispute and the pursuit of either contention tends to arouse the discussion of two key problems: the definition must be broad enough to encompass essential elements common to all religions, but it must not be so expansive as to embrace every type of secular meaning system and value orientation.

Defining Religion

Nevertheless, for all the problems of the many definitions offered, they contain a common core that yields an essential element. There is consensus that the thing we are trying to understand always has some primary relevance to questions about "ultimate meaning" of the existential basics: Is there a purpose to existence? Why are we here? What can we hope? Is death the end? Why do we suffer? Does justice exist? Not all answers to these questions are religious, but only those that assume the existence of the *supernatural* —forces beyond or outside nature, an unknowable realm that can alter, suspend, or ignore physical forces. A further postulate is that this force is active, that events and conditions here on earth are influenced by the supernatural.[4]

Let us approach this definitional problem in another way because we need an understanding of the undefined term *ultimate meaning*. Human beings seek explanations; they want to know what rewards may be obtained and what costs are incurred. It is important to realize that we do not

3

here conceive of rewards in a narrow and materialistic way. Some desired rewards are very scarce, including some that cannot be definitely shown to exist at all, or lie in the distant future or in some other non-verifiable context. This insight brings us to the key concept—compensators—on which our theory of religion turns: *Compensators are postulations of reward according to explanations that are not readily susceptible to unambiguous evaluation.* They are not in any way pejorative, but they are based in hope and faith rather than in knowledge, although sometimes hope is fulfilled and faith is redeemed.

Compensators may be broken down along several dimensions. One useful distinction is between relatively *specific* and relatively *general* compensators. This follows the distinction often made in behavioral psychology between specific and general reinforcers or rewards.[5] A specific compensator substitutes for a specific reward; that is, it claims to provide something of limited value and narrow scope. For example, an antibiotic treatment for an infection is a specific reward, while a magical potion taken in the same circumstances is a specific compensator. General compensators are substitutes for very general rewards (such as "health") and for large collections of rewards. For example, "heaven" is a very general compensator that implies an unlimited flow of varied rewards.

Solutions to questions of ultimate meaning seem only available in the form of compensators. Consider the question: What is the goal of history? To answer is to make a statement that is beyond verification, unless perhaps in the far distant future. Furthermore, some questions of ultimate meaning can be answered only by assuming the existence of the supernatural. For example, for history to have a goal, some conscious being must have set that goal. Only a supernatural being could have the vantage point and the power to establish a goal for history.

It is obvious that religion is a major source of general

compensators, and that any particular religion organizes its compensators into a system. Indeed, the most general compensators entail explanations concerning ultimate meaning. It follows, therefore, that the more standard definition of religion we discussed above can be translated into the following form: *A religion is a system of general compensators based on supernatural assumptions.* Limited space makes it impossible to demonstrate the full merits of this definition in the present paper. Elsewhere, we derive this definition from basic elements of our core theory.[6] Using this translation, we are able to derive a very large number of quite complex propositions about religious phenomena, including why and how religious movements form and why and how they thrive or flounder. Based on an analysis of exchange processes, and clarifying what is exchanged, this definition permits us a clearer vision of what actually is going on in religious organizations.

Attributes and Correlates

The conceptual literature on churches and sects is dominated by typologies. Indeed, the literature commonly refers not to churches and sects, but to the "church-sect typology." Sad to say, the *kind* of types usually developed by sociologists are of no use in theory construction—they serve as tautological substitutes for real theories and tend to prevent theorizing. The trouble started with Max Weber who introduced both the church-sect typology and a misunderstanding of the ideal type. In his classic work on methods, he advocated the construction of ideal types:

> by the one-sided *accentuation* of one or more points of view and by the synthesis of a great many diffuse, discrete, more or less present and occasionally absent *concrete individual* phenomena, which are arranged according to these one-sidedly emphasized viewpoints into a unified *analytical* construct. In its conceptual purity, this mental construct cannot be found anywhere in reality.... They are used as

conceptual instruments for *comparison* with and the *measurement* of reality.[7]

Generations of sociologists have regarded Weber's ideal type as similar to concepts commonly found in the physical sciences. Physics, for example, abounds with "ideal gasses" and "frictionless states," which are nonexistent but are the absolute base points on a measuring continuum against which degrees of friction or the expansion of gasses can be calibrated. But there is an immense and fatal difference between these ideal types and those proposed and compounded by Weber. The ideal types of physics *anchor a single continuum along which it is possible to rank order all empirical or hypothetical cases.* Comparison with the ideal is direct and unambiguous and thus permits measurement. Weber's types prevent comparison and measurement, despite his claim that "they are indispensable for this purpose."

Following Weber, sociologists often use *correlates* in their definitions of concepts, but it is *attributes,* not correlates, that belong in a definition. Consider the most minimal use of a definition: to permit clear identification of cases as belonging or not belonging to the defined class. Since correlates are not always present—and often may not be present—their use as defining features often leads to misclassification. Worse yet, when many correlates are involved (as Weber advised they should be), the result is a jumble of mixed types which cannot be ordered and thus which cannot yield measurement. The usual outcome is a proliferation of new subconcepts of types, and sometimes it seems that each new empirical case must become a unique type—which is to classify nothing.

When *attributes* are the basis of definition (since they are always present in the phenomena to be classified) and when enough attributes have been utilized to limit the class in the desired fashion, no ambiguity results. For then the concept forms an underlying *unidimensional* axis of variation. This kind of ideal type, then, does provide a zero point for comparison and ranking.

Churches and Movements

Although Weber introduced the notions of church and sect, it was his student Ernst Troeltsch who first made them important. He used an ideal type of church and an ideal type of sect to categorize roughly what he regarded as the two main varieties of religious bodies in pre-nineteenth century Christian Europe. Each type was identified by a host of characteristics which were, at best, weak correlates of one another and of the phenomena to be classified.[8] Subsequent attempts to utilize Troeltsch's types in other times and places caused frustration. The empirical cases just did not fit well, so new users created new church-sect typologies. Indeed, it would be close to the truth to claim that *each* new user, or at least each new user with new cases to classify, created a new typology based on different correlated features of the phenomena to be classified. And each new typology suffered the same defects as those it replaced: it could not organize the data.

Underlying most sociologists' interest in churches and sects is a theory about religious movements. In 1929 H. Richard Niebuhr argued that the sect is an unstable type of religious organization which, through time, tends to be transformed into a church. But, he argued, following this transformation, many members' needs that had been satisfied by the sect go unmet by the church.[9] In time this leads to discontent, which prompts schism and the splitting off of a new sect, which then is transformed slowly into a church, thus to spawn a new sect: an endless cycle of birth, transformation, schism, and rebirth of religious movements.

It is this theory that has long captivated sociologists of religion. The trouble is that a typological conception of churches and sects prevents all theorizing. How can one theorize about the movement from sect to church when one cannot rank groups as more or less churchlike? It would humble theorists to try to theorize under such handicaps.

Thus it was an event of considerable magnitude when Benton Johnson proposed a vast definitional rummage sale. He discarded dozens of correlates from the various definitions of church and sect and settled on a single attribute to classify religious groups: *"A church is a religious group that accepts the social environment in which it exists. A sect is a religious group that rejects the social environment in which it exists."*[10]

What Johnson did was to postulate a continuum representing the degree to which a religious group was in a *state of tension* with its surrounding sociocultural environment. The ideal sect falls at one pole where the surrounding tension is so great that sect members are hunted fugitives. The ideal church anchors the other end of the continuum and virtually *is* the sociocultural environment—the two are so merged that it is impossible to postulate a basis for tension. Johnson's ideal types, unlike Weber's, are ideal in precisely the same way that ideal gasses and frictionless states are ideal. They identify a clear axis of variation and its end points. Johnson's reconceptualization also permits clear definition of two other important concepts: religious *movement* and religious *institution*. When we look at the low tension end of his axis we find not only churches, we find religious *institutions*. That is, we find a stable sector of social structure, a cluster of roles, norms, values, and activities associated with the performance of key social functions.

Social institutions are not social movements—if we define social movements as *organized groups* whose primary goal is to *cause* or *prevent* social change.[11] Institutions adapt to change. Social movements seek to alter or to become institutions. Thus we can see that if religious institutions are one pole of the tension axis, as we move along the axis in the direction of greater tension we discover religious movements. We realize then that religious movements are social movements that wish to cause or prevent change in a system of beliefs, values, symbols, and practices concerned with providing supernaturally-based general compensators. In a very general way it can be asserted that religious movements are organized groups wishing to become religious institutions. Such groups would like to become the dominant faith in their society, although they may make little effort to achieve this end if they are convinced their chances are too remote.

Johnson's axis also permits us to characterize the direction taken by religious movements. When they move toward less tension with their sociocultural environment they are *church movements* (although a group may remain a sect during a long period of movement in this churchlike direction). When groups move towards the high tension pole they are *sect movements*. We are now working on another paper to show that the *degree of tension* experienced by a religious group can be measured easily and unambiguously. We also explain that tension with the sociocultural environment is equivalent to *subcultural deviance* in which the relationship between the high tension group and the surrounding society is marked by *difference, antagonism,* and *separation*—three integrated but conceptually distinguishable aspects of deviance. Since tension defined in this way can be measured, numerous empirical studies can now readily be performed, testing any hypothesis or theory in which tension plays a part.

The utility of Johnson's reconceptualization of church and sect is obvious. For example, we may now see at a glance that the Catholic Church in the United States is more sectlike than is the Catholic Church in Ireland. In most prior typologies this could not be seen. Furthermore, because the axis of variation is clear, variation cries out for explanation. It becomes obvious now how to proceed towards theories to rectify and extend Niebuhr's work. Indeed, many important variables long thought to influence the generation of sects, or their transformation into churches, can now be examined. In the past, these variables have been utilized in typologizing and thus were locked in tautology. Now we can ask, for example, if the arrival of a generation of members socialized into the sect as children, rather than converted into it as adults, plays a major role in pushing sects down the road to churchliness. In the past this variable was lost in the creation of (1) sects with converted members, (2) sects with socialized members, (3) churches with converted members, and (4) churches with socialized members. These four boxes tell us nothing. A proposition that related socialization to the transformation of sects into churches could tell us much.

At first glance it may appear that Johnson has taken the necessary steps to develop the conceptual means for theorizing about religious groups. Unfortunately he did not do so. There are at least *two kinds* of religious movements in a high state of tension with their surrounding sociocultural environment, and it demonstrably inhibits efficient theorizing to regard both kinds as sects, and ignore the differences between them. We must, therefore, now add some complexity to Johnson's elegant parsimony.

Niebuhr's theory exclusively concerns *schismatic* religious movements, which he identified as sects. He was not speaking of all small, deviant religious movements, but only of those whose existence began as an internal faction of another religious body. This is, of course, a very common kind of religious movement. It is not, however, the only kind of religious movement in a high state of tension with the surrounding sociocultural environment. Many such movements have no history of prior organizational attachment to a "parent" religion—thus they are not schismatic. Indeed, they lack a close cultural continuity with (or similarity to) other religious groups in their society. These non-schismatic, deviant religious groups are themselves of two types. One type represents cultural *innovation.* That is, along with the many familiar components of religious culture appearing in the beliefs, values, symbols, and practices of the group, there is something distinctive and new about them as well.

The second type exhibits cultural *importation*. Such groups represent (or claim to represent) a religious body well-established in another society. Examples are various far-eastern faiths in the United States, or Christianity in the Far East. In common parlance, these deviant but non-schismatic bodies often are referred to as *cults*.[12]

Sects and Cults

These preliminary remarks can be expanded to define sects and cults, both of which are deviant religious bodies— that is, they are in a state of relatively high tension with their surrounding sociocultural environment. Sects, however, have a *prior tie with another religious organization*. To be a sect, a religious movement must have been founded by persons who left another religious body *for the purpose* of founding the sect. The term *sect*, therefore, applies only to schismatic movements. Note that this definition does *not* require that a sect *break off from a church*, as Niebuhr argued. To insist on this would land us back in the wilderness of typologies, for sects sometimes break off from other sects. Indeed, it has happened that churches have broken off from sects.[13] Furthermore, we plan to apply elements of church-sect theory to the careers of cults. These are matters, therefore, to theorize about, not to lock into definitions.

Because sects are schismatic groups they present themselves to the world as something *old*. They left the parent body not to form a new faith but to *reestablish the old one*, from which the parent body had ''drifted''(usually by becoming more churchlike). Sects claim to be the authentic, purged, refurbished version of the faith from which they split. Luther, for example, did not claim to be leading a new church but the true church cleansed of worldly encrustations. *Cults*, with the exception we shall note, *do not have a prior tie* with another religious body in the society where they exist. The cult may represent an alien (external) religion, or it may have originated in the host society—but through innovation, not fission.

Whether domestic or imported, the cult is something *new* vis-à-vis the other religious bodies in the society in question. If domestic—regardless of how much of the common religious culture it retains—the cult adds to that culture a new revelation or insight justifying the claim that it is different, new, more advanced. Imported cults seldom share a common culture with the existing faiths. While they may be old in some other society, they are new and different in the importing society.

Cults, then, represent an *independent religious tradition* in a society. In time they may become the dominant tradition, in which case there is no longer much tension between them and the environment, and they become the church or churches of that society. Even long before cults become churches, they too are prone to internal schisms. Thus, within the context of cult movements, schismatic movements *can form.* A theory to explain sect formation can then be applied to cults to explain their schismatic tendencies. But it is vital to see that a theory of sect formation simply *will not serve as a theory of cult formation.* The geneses of the two are very different. It is clear then that sects are breeds of a common species; cults are a different species and occur by mutation or migration. Sects, being schismatic, are embodied in religious organizations, and their status as religious movements is clear. Many cults, however, do not develop into full-blown religious movements. It is necessary, therefore, to survey the range of cults to identify various forms, only some of which will fall within the scope of a theory of religious movements.

Audience Cults

Three degrees of organization (or lack of organization) characterize cults. The most diffuse and least organized kind of cult could be best identified as an *audience.* Sometimes some members of this audience actually may gather to hear a lecture. But there are virtually no aspects of formal organization to these activities, and membership remains at most a consumer activity. Indeed, cult audiences often do not gather physically but consume cult doctrines entirely through magazines, books, newspapers, radio and television.

In 1960 John Lofland and Rodney Stark initiated a research study of cult movements.[14] In 1970 William Bainbridge began a similar search for cult activities and groups.[15] Our initial discovery was that the bulk of cult activity is not connected to organized cult movements. To the degree that it involves face-to-face interaction at all (as opposed to reliance on mass communications media), it most closely resembles a very loose lecture circuit. Persons with a cult doctrine to offer rely on advertisements, publicity, and direct mail to assemble an audience to hear their lectures. Almost invariably at these lectures efforts are made to sell ancillary materials—books, magazines, souvenirs, and the like—but no significant efforts are attempted to organize the audience.

These public gatherings are often of the most unsystematic and flexible character. The description of a typical "Space Craft Convention," held during the early sixties, illustrates this point. About five hundred persons registered for this annual convention held regularly in Oakland, California, for the alleged purpose of seriously exchanging information and research findings about flying saucers (UFOs). Approximately twenty speakers were scheduled over each two-day convention. And many others with a cult message set up booths.

Some of these speakers devoted their time to describing their own *trips* into outer space on flying saucers that were piloted by persons from other planets! Some of these speakers even displayed (and sold) photographs of the saucer on which they had made the journey, and of outer-space pilots who had taken them for the ride. What seemed astounding in context—since the tales told by those who had been contacted by spacemen seemed to be accepted uncritically—was the fact that other speakers spent their time trying merely to demonstrate that some kind of Unidentified Flying Objects *must exist,* but without claiming that they necessarily came from outer space. People who had, during the previous hour, given nodding support to tales of space travelers also gave full attention to those who were merely suggesting that saucers might exist. Moreover, a great many speakers (and the majority of those working out of booths) had little connection with the saucer question at all. Instead they promoted standard varieties of pseudo-science and occult doctrines on the grounds that these flourish on the more enlightened worlds from which UFOs come. Astrologers, medical quacks, inventors of perpetual motion machines (seeking investors), food faddists, spiritualists, and the like were all present and busy.

Conversations with many in attendance at Space Craft Conventions revealed that these people were not the stuff of which social movements can be made. They accepted everything, more or less, and in effect accepted nothing— they were "interested" in all new ideas in the general area of the eccentric and the mystical. Their sheer openmindedness apparently made it impossible for them to develop a strong commitment to any complete system of thought; they were constitutional "nibblers." The fact is that several speakers at these conventions wanted to found cult movements, but their efforts to create organization met with no significant success. Later observation within several cult movements taught us that the leaders of such movements soon learn to avoid the cult audiences in their search for converts. It is easy to get a hearing from such persons, but serious commitment is almost never forthcoming.

Nevertheless, people who attend events like the Space Craft Convention are among the most committed and active members of cult audiences. Perhaps the great majority of persons who presently give credence to ideas that are defined as cult doctrines in American society do so almost entirely through impersonal communications. They read astrology columns and books. They swell the circulation of the *National Enquirer* and other publications that give play to psychics, biorhythms, spiritualism, UFOs, and similar pseudo-scientific, mystical, meaning systems. While many people who end up in cult movements also seem to have once been part of this audience, few members of the audience ever are recruited into a cult movement.

Client Cults

More organized than audience cults are collectivities that can be characterized as *client cults*. Here the relationship between those promulgating cult doctrine and those partaking of it most closely resembles the relationship between therapist and patient, or between consultant and client. Considerable organization may be found among those *offering* the cult service, but clients remain little organized. Furthermore, no successful effort is expended to weld the clients into a social movement. Indeed, client involvement is so partial that clients often retain an active commitment to another religious movement or institution.

Some cults manage to become service and therapy occupations. In the past the primary services sold were medical miracles, forecasts of the future, or contact with the dead. Since Freud, however, cults increasingly have specialized in personal adjustment. Thus, today one can "get it" at *est,* get "cleared" through Scientology, store up orgone and seek the monumental orgasm through the Reich Foundation, get rolfed, actualized, sensitized, or psychoanalyzed.

What is important to recognize about cults of this type is that, while they mobilize participants much more fully than do the audience cults, their mobility is *partial* rather than all-embracing. Most participants remain clients, not members. Some of them participate in two or more cults simultaneously, although with greater involvement than is usual in cult audiences. And quite often clients of these cults retain their participation in an organized religious group. In our travels through the cult world we found that many people who frequented spiritualist groups went regularly to a conventional church come Sunday morning. It seems significant that they usually went to churches, not sects. As we shall see, sects are much more hostile than are churches to groups with religious implications that are external to the sect. Indeed, it is not uncommon for clergy from conventional churches to frequent various client cults, particularly those of the personal adjustment variety, apparently feeling little stress from their dual involvements.

Cult Movements

Finally, there are *cult movements* which can be distinguished from other religious movements only in terms of the distinctions we have developed between cults and sects. It is only cult movements that will be addressed in our subsequent theory. However, the less organized types are currently more common and need to be described with some care so that they are not confused with the full-fledged cult movement.

When a spiritualist medium is able to get his or her clients to attend sessions regularly on Sunday morning, and thus in a Christian context to sever their ties with other religious organizations, we observe the birth of a cult *movement.* Cult movements are fully-fledged religious organizations which attempt to satisfy all the religious needs of converts. Dual membership with any other faith is out. Attempts to cause social change, by converting others to membership, become central to the group agenda.

Nevertheless, cult movements differ considerably in the degree to which they attempt to mobilize their members and to usher in the "New Age." Many cult movements are very weak organizations. They are essentially study groups who gather regularly to hear discussions of the new revelations or latest spirit messages gained by the leader. Little more than modest financial support, attendance at group functions, and assent to the truth of the cult doctrines, is asked of members. Frequently the group observes no moral prohibitions more restrictive than those of the general society. Unless an outsider gets into a religious discussion with members, no indication of their religious deviance is likely to be evident. On the other hand, some cult movements function much like conventional sects. Levels of member commitment are quite intense, tension with the outside world is high (moral prohibitions exceed those of the general society), but participation is only partial. That is, most members continue to lead regular secular lives—they work, marry, rear children, have hobbies, take vacations, and have contact in the ordinary way with non-cult members such as family and friends.

There are some cult movements, however, that demand much more. They are a total way of life. They require members to dispense with their secular lives and devote themselves entirely to the activities of the cult. Such members become, in Philip Selznick's felicitous expression, "deployable agents."[16] Their lives are circumscribed wholly by the demands of the cult. Usually they live in communities and if they hold jobs it will be only where and when they are directed to do so, often in enterprises owned and operated by the cult. Today it is common for cult members to support themselves and their movements as mendicants on the streets, sometimes selling books, pamphlets, charms, or even candy and flowers for a "donation."[17] Most people would be very surprised at how much money a small number of deployable agents can raise in this way on the streets, and perhaps this is one reason why cults are so likely to adopt this strategy. When not engaged in fundraising, these deployable agents give testimony, seek converts, devote themselves to group chores or worship activities. From a modern secular perspective this requirement for mendicancy may limit the growth of the group while it increases tension with the "outside world."

Our three "types" of cults can be distinguished in terms of the qualities of the compensators they provide. Thus, rather than being three "unideal types," they are merely convenient words to describe particular ranges in measurement scales on dimensions we have already introduced. Audience cults are identified by the low value, and consequent low cost, of the compensators they provide. Our two other types are points along a *continuum* defined by the degree of *generality of the compensators* offered by a given cult. Audience cults offer very vague and weak compensators, often little more than a mild vicarious thrill or social entertainment. Client cults offer valued but relatively *specific* compensators. Psychoanalysis and Dianetics claim to cure neurosis, but they do not promise everlasting life. Cult movements present a much larger package of compensators, including the most *general* compensators offered by full-fledged sects and churches.

These three levels of cults can also be described conveniently in traditional terms: audience cults provide *mythology;* client cults add serious *magic;* cult movements are true *religions.* Put another way, not all cults are religions in the strict sense of the term because not all represent systems of ultimate meaning. Audience cults are part of a diffuse occult milieu that toys with vague images of the ultimate. Also within this milieu are many unsuccessful client cults and cult movements, including many one-person operations with no committed followers. But, in themselves, audience cults offer only very limited rewards and compensators.

Client cults are *magical* rather than *religious.* This means that their main business is selling compensators rather than rewards, and the compensators are relatively specific and not embodied in a total system of ultimate meaning. Freud does not tell us how our lives are meaningfully related to the ultimate laws of the universe, but he does provide specific meanings to attach to limited aspects of the human condition. Our distinction between magic and religion is entirely in line with some of the best traditional descriptions of these two related expressions of human desire.[18]

Genuine Cultic Religion

Only *cult* movements are genuinely religious in the fullest sense, although some of them may not accept the label of "religion." One may debate the proper conceptual boundary between religious cults and other cult-like phenomena, especially magical, service organizations. This debate has raged in the courts in recent years as various groups (such as Scientology, the Black Muslims, and Transcendental Meditation) have struggled to obtain, or avoid, legal definition as religious organizations. One of the advantages of our definition of *cult* is that it explains why this debate has taken place. Because cults are culturally novel or exotic, the conventional definitions of our society do not automatically apply to them. When a sect breaks away from a church, it takes with it the label "religious," but cults are not born with the religious label attached.

Under our definitions of "cult" and "religion" the analytical concept of compensators makes good sense out of the otherwise bewildering variety of cults. Only those cults that offer quite general compensators (a system of ultimate meanings) fully qualify as religious. Our conceptualization also transforms what has been a swamp of unproductive debate into a fruitful field for scientific research. Recall Niebuhr's observation that sects tend to evolve into churches. Our research indicates that magical client cults tend to evolve into religious cult movements. Although examples abound, the best documented are Scientology and "The Power."[19] Both groups began as limited psychotherapy services. Because they were culturally novel and were not based on any body of verified scientific research, they were magical client cults rather than technical medical services. As the years passed, each of these two cults began to offer compensators that were more and more general and for which no equivalent rewards existed. Their ideologies ramified into complex systems of ultimate meaning. Now, both are highly developed cult movements.

Within our conceptual framework we can also apply to cults many of the ideas originally developed in the understanding of sects and churches. For example, we may discuss the degree of tension that a cult experiences with the surrounding society. It would appear that cults can enjoy relatively low tension with their environment as long as they do not organize into religious movements. Participating in cult audiences seems to be a very low risk activity. A Gallup Poll in 1976 suggests that twenty-two percent of Americans believe in astrology; and astrology columns and publications flourish, but very little criticism is directed toward astrology. In general, the clergy of American churches seem to ignore the astrology cult. At most, persons who participate in audience cults may risk censure from those immediately around them.

Client cults, too, do not provoke great hostility in the surrounding sociocultural environment. As long as they do not run afoul of fraud statutes (by selling building lots on a fictitious planet, for example) or licensing statutes governing medical practice, they are not subject to much harassment. Client cults seem also never to serve a low status market, if for no other reason than that they charge for their services. Consequently, client cults also seem to be somewhat protected by the high status of their clientele. For example, the spiritualists have drawn primarily on middle and upper class clientele, as do most of today's personal adjustment cults, and this seems to have lent them considerable protection from opposition.

It is when cults become religious movements that their environment heats up. For example, as Scientology evolved from a client cult to a movement seeking major commitment from members, its legal troubles grew. In similar fashion, Transcendental Meditation took little heat so long as it concentrated on teaching clients to meditate during a few training sessions. With its transformation into an intense religious movement—amid claims that advanced members could fly (levitate)—public reaction has grown. And it is cult movements, not client cults or audiences, that today face opposition from irate parents who hire deprogrammers to kidnap their children from the bosom of the cult.

Furthermore, among cult movements, the more a cult mobilizes its membership, the greater the opposition it engenders. Cults whose members remain in the society to pursue normal lives and occupations engender much less opposition than do cults whose members drop everything to become full-time converts. In part, this is probably because cults that function as total institutions rupture converts' ties to conventional institutions. This generates personal grievances against the movement. It is one thing to know your son or daughter, for example, attends a weird church and has odd beliefs, but it is quite something else to lose contact with a child who takes up full-time participation in an alien faith. Indeed, even Catholic parents often find it painful to lose a child to a convent or monastery even though the question of deviant faith is not an issue. Thus the rule seems to be: the more total the movement, the more total the opposition to it.

Summary and Conclusions

Concepts must not only facilitate theorizing; they ought to inspire it. Concepts should identify a phenomenon that arouses our interest and should present a clear enough picture of the phenomenon's variation so that we are prompted to explain it. We believe the conceptual scheme developed above does encourage such theory construction. To conclude this paper, therefore, let us point out some basic questions thrown into relief by these particular formulations— basic questions that must be answered by any adequate theory of religious movements.

The most obvious task is to seek a set of premises from which a theory of religious *schism* can be deduced. Why and under what conditions do factions form in a religious group? Why and when do these factions split off to form a sect movement? A church movement? Under what conditions do schismatic forces produce secular rather than religious movements? This last question reminds us that we must theorize not merely about the internal workings of religious bodies, but we must also deal with their external environment. Thus, for example, we need to know not only how sects form within a parent body, but the social conditions under which religious schisms are more likely, or less likely.

In posing these questions we are permitted, by the nature of our concepts, to avoid the assumption that sects split off from churches. Instead, we are directed to the problem of faction and exodus in *any* kind of religious body. This is important because the historical record makes clear that sect formation is probably more common within bodies that are themselves sects rather than churches. It also permits analysis of schismatic movements originating in cults, just as it lets us deal with church movements that have split off from sects or cults. Instead of converting these alternatives into un-ideal types, our conceptual scheme makes it possible to construct propositions to account for these variations.

Our conceptual framework makes it clear that a theory of religious schism pertains to only some religious movements. Cults are not the result of schism (although, once founded, cults become subject to schism). A theory of cult formation, therefore, may have very few propositions in common with a theory of religious schism (a term to be preferred to sect-formation because it is more inclusive). We must explain when the sociocultural environment is conducive to cult formation, and why. We must also specify the process by which people actually form a cult, and we must explain the contingencies governing importation of cults.

The next requirement is the need for a theory of development and transformation. Once a sect or cult is formed, what contingencies govern whether it will grow, stall, or fail? What factors operate to push it in a church-like direction (toward lower tension)? What factors push it toward higher tension? Finally, we must close the circle by showing how and to what extent the factors involved in the formation of religious groups influence their development and transformation, and how these in turn are involved in the onset of schism and of cult formation and importation. This is, of course, a formidable list, but with the conceptual clarifications at hand we have identified some propositions which enable us to deduce at least partial answers to many of these questions.

In conclusion we would like to suggest that it is important for sociologists to pursue such a theory. One virtue of this pursuit is relevant to a comment made by Ellsworth Faris a half-century ago: The origin of many social institutions and much human culture "is lost in mystery." We have no time machine to permit study of the past. But religious sects and cults can be studied from the start and can thus furnish a body of information "concerning the rise of institutions," and the invention of culture.[20] Social scientists have always envied the geneticists' rapidly reproducing fruit flies. We suggest that for a great many sociological questions the cult and sect provide a reasonable substitute.

Unfortunately, we have not made much theoretical progress towards explaining religious movements since 1929 when Niebuhr sketched his church-sect theory and when Ellsworth Faris published a one-page, eight-point directive listing urgent business for sociological study. Two of his points are relevant to our discussion: First, "a sociological study of the origin and evolution of specific religious sects ought to be very fruitful in making us intelligent about how institutions arise and develop. The study of sects which have disappeared and of those whose birth was abortive would be highly instructive." Second, "the study of social movements should include significant religious movements. There are social, racial, and economic aspects which do not appear at all in the controversial literature."[21]

Since Faris wrote those lines, many sects and cults have been studied ethnographically, but theoretical progress was stifled by ill-advised attempts to find a set of boxes in which to place each religious movement. Built of correlates, the sets of boxes expanded endlessly. Everything was named. Nothing was explained. We believe it is time to use this mass of rich observations for the purpose of theory-construction and theory-testing. These pages have been offered as a step in that direction.

NOTES

1 This chapter is a revision of our earlier article, "Of Churches, Sects, and Cults: Preliminary Concepts for a Theory of Religious Movements," *Journal for the Scientific Study of Religion*, 18, no. 2 (June 1979): 117-31.

2 Peter Berger, *The Sacred Canopy* (Garden City, N.Y.: Doubleday, 1967). See also Jack Goody, "Religion and Ritual: The Definitional Problem," *British Journal of Sociology*, 12, no. 2 (June 1961): 142-64.

3 For example, see Robert Bellah, "Christianity and Symbolic Realism," *Journal for the Scientific Study of Religion*, 9, no. 2 (Summer 1970): 89-96; also J. Milton Yinger, *The Scientific Study of Religion* (New York: Macmillan, 1970).

4 See the discussion in Rodney Stark, "Must All Religions be Supernatural?" in Bryan Wilson, ed., *The Social Impact of New Religious Movements*, (Barrytown, N.Y.: Unification Theological Seminary, distr. Rose of Sharon Press, 1981), pp. 159-77.

5 See George Homans, *Social Behavior: Its Elementary Forms* (New York: Harcourt Brace, 1974), p. 29.

6 Rodney Stark and William Sims Bainbridge, "Towards a Theory of Religion: Religious Commitment," *Journal for the Scientific Study of Religion*, 19, no. 2 (June 1980): 114-28.

7 Max Weber, *The Methodology of the Social Sciences* (Glencoes: The Free Press, 1949), pp. 91-97.

8 Ernst Troeltsch, *The Social Teaching of the Christian Churches* (New York: Macmillan, 1931).

9 H. Richard Niebuhr, *The Social Sources of Denominationalism* (New York: Henry Holt, 1929).

10 Benton Johnson, "On Church and Sect," *American Sociological Review*, 28, no. 4 (August 1963): 539-49.

11 See William Sims Bainbridge, "Collective Behavior and Social Movements," in Rodney Stark, *Sociology* (New York: Worth, 1979).

12 Allan W. Eister, "An Outline of a Structural Theory of Cults," *Journal for the Scientific Study of Religion*, 11, no. 4 (December 1972): 319-33.

13 See Stephen Steinberg, "Reform Judaism: The Origin and Evolution of a 'church movement,'" *Journal for the Scientific Study of Religion*, 5, no. 1 (October 1965): 117-29.

14 See John Lofland and Rodney Stark, "Becoming a World-saver: A Theory of Conversion to a Deviant Perspective," *American Sociological Review*, 30, no. 6 (December 1965): 862-75.

15 William Sims Bainbridge, *Satan's Power* (Berkeley: University of California Press, 1978).

16 Philip Selznick, *The Organizational Weapon* (Glencoe: The Free Press, 1960).

17 See David G. Bromley and Anson D. Shupe, Jr., *Moonies in America: Cult, Church and Crusade* (Beverley Hills: Sage, 1979).

18 See Emile Durkheim, *The Elementary Forms of the Religious Life* (London: George Allen and Unwin, 1915).

19 On Scientology see Roy Wallis, *The Road to Total Freedom* (New York: Columbia University Press, 1976). See also William Sims Bainbridge, *Satan's Power*.

20 Ellsworth Faris, "The Sect and the Sectarian," *American Journal of Sociology*, 60 (Supplement, 1955): 75-89.

21 Ellsworth Faris, "Some Phases of Religion that are Susceptible of Sociological Study," *American Journal of Sociology*, 60 (Supplement, 1955): 90.

A Definition of Cult: Terms and Approaches

David Martin

In what follows I offer a critical but sympathetic commentary on a major article by Stark and Bainbridge entitled "Of Churches, Sects, and Cults," appearing in the *Journal for the Scientific Study of Religion*.[1] Since the article is rich and wide-ranging I can select only certain key elements for attention. Thus, I entirely omit the important section on the definition of religion. My point of departure is rather the section which deals with the principles of conceptualization and the way these bear on how we should understand and utilize such fundamental terms as "church" and "cult." In discussing principles of conceptualization, I concentrate on the heuristic use of the term "church." Thereafter, I turn more specifically to the proposals which Stark and Bainbridge make with respect to "cult."

Correlative Concepts

Stark and Bainbridge hold that concepts should not be composed of correlates. In their view, to construct concepts out of correlates is to presuppose what has still to be shown, that is, the relationship between variables. Their object is rather to find a single parsimonious variable as the basis for distinguishing the concepts classically deployed in the sociology of religion. The variable they select is the degree of tension with the *status quo,* as Benton Johnson earlier argued that a church accepts the social environment in which it exists while the sect rejects it.[2] Of course, nobody would want to quarrel with a selection insofar as it represents one viable research tactic among others. Whether it is the most viable tactic is, however, open to question, and whether it is the only viable tactic is more than questionable. Nevertheless, Stark and Bainbridge write as if the subject has been seriously retarded by refusal to adopt their approved method of conceptualization. I would like, therefore, to indicate just how the method of using concepts embodying correlates can be deployed in practice, without losing sight of the empirical mix found in the "real world." Social phenomena can be "come at" from a wide variety of angles, though if genuine science is involved, there should be some convergence in results over the long run.

I had myself always understood our concepts as made up of things usually observed to go together, which means, I suppose, that they are correlated: co-related. They belong together more often than not. This means that they are interim generalizations, tied up in a preliminary way within the boundaries of the concept. If I say, for example, that a church tends to accept the broad alignments of power and status within a given society, I itemize one element in the type, or concept. I may then go on to say that a church generally has a body of ritual experts, who are themselves guardians of the sacred, and who are part of a hierarchy of power and status. From that point, I can develop the concept a little further and suggest that this ecclesiastical hierarchy will be analogous to, or perhaps parallel with, the secular hierarchy. The secular and ecclesiastical alignments of power and status will run in parallel and will tend to be mutually supportive.

More elements could be adduced but that brief characterization provides the nub of what is needed for a concept, or type. More should be said in response to Stark and Bainbridge's criticism that such types "serve as tautological substitutes for real theories."[3] I do not see that this is a tautology. Indeed, insofar as it is concerned with co-relationships, it could not possibly be tautologous. As I understand the term, tautology involves a complete, unbreakable definitional circle, or as philosophers would say "an analytic truth." The kind of formulation just put forward is *not* analytically true.

However, there are elements within the definition which do contain a *socio*logic, and this *socio*logic involves relationships very powerfully interwoven and interlocked. Let me illustrate. The definition began with a reference to the fact that a church accepts the current disposition of power and status. Nobody can argue with *that* because I am simply saying how I intend to deploy a word. However, I also say that the system of power within the church will be cross-referenced against the system of power within the society. The church hierarchy will support the social hierarchy and in return the social hierarchy will support the church.

This needs and invites careful scrutiny. It is not, as I've already suggested, tautologous, since this mutual support is not a necessary truth. It exhibits separate elements in an empirical relationship. Yet so far as the sociologic is concerned, there is a *near*-inevitability about the relationship. It would be surprising, to say the least, if one hierarchy supported another without the slightest reciprocity. The definition as formulated leans on a plausible logic of reciprocal support. It might seem difficult to imagine the absence of such reciprocity. But it is part of a scientific approach to try.

Church-State Reciprocity

Let us try. We might perform the mental experiment of imagining a bench of bishops (or for that matter a Synod of godly presbyters) who backed the social order in general but were repudiated by the incumbents of the key positions in the social hierarchy. Immediately we perform the experiment, a case comes to mind. The Russian Orthodox Church supports the social order, not merely with enthusiasm, but obsequiously. Yet it does not receive support in return. There is a certain minimal reciprocity, since it receives more support and recognition than the Baptists and much more than the dissident Baptists and the Jehovah's Witnesses, but one cannot really speak of mutual support. The alignment of secular power which the church supports is so tipped against religion that symmetrical mutuality is excluded, just as a religiously motivated protest also is almost excluded.

Let us also try to see what other instance may be adduced where reciprocity does not obtain. The article by Stark and Bainbridge mentions the Roman Catholic Church in Ireland as a very strong instance of what is meant by a church. However, until 1922 the religious hierarchy was not well-disposed towards the social hierarchy, nor was the structure of power all that favorable to the Roman Catholic Church. Nevertheless, the church was a very conservative body, and generally opposed to social changes in a thoroughly churchly manner, except one, which was Irish independence. It was not in tension with its environment: indeed, church and environment were virtually identical. This church was exactly the same after 1922, and it is precisely this church which comprises the minority in Northern Ireland, one and the same both sides of the border.

So what? Why adduce these examples where the powerful, interwoven sociologic encapsulated in our definition does not hold? I certainly do not adduce these examples to suggest that the sociologic in the definition is less powerful than it seems. The reciprocity of ecclesiastical and secular orders is an important part of the definition and it remains based on sociological rules capable of sustained exposition. The rationale of adducing such examples is rather to draw attention to the important issues which a definition can open up. A definition by presenting to the mind certain postulated leakages invites the search for exceptions, and these exceptions then create an illuminating dialectic with the original definition.

The dialectic needs to be pursued a little to see what it yields. The first exception was the Russian Orthodox Church. This conformed to the first element in the definition, relating support of the social order, but contradicted what seems a reasonable, powerful extrapolation within that definition about the mutual support given to each other by social and ecclesiastical hierarchies. In Russia there is conspicuous asymmetry. Why? One reason relates to the influence which

the social hierarchy exercises on those who actually constitute the episcopate. This arises partly because it is a totali-
tarian regime, but also in part because that regime inherited
the practices and assumptions of the previous social order,
where social and ecclesiastical elites *were,* indeed, mutually
supportive, and where reciprocity included a great deal of
state influence on who was appointed Bishop and how Bishops exercised their functions.

Put in another way, the Russian situation exemplifies
that lack of radical criticism of the social order which was
the first element in our definition. Yet it lacked the mutual
support of social and ecclesiastical elites which was postulated in more extended parts of the definition. An examination of that lack reveals how the historical inertia of a previous regime, operative till 1917, can be utilized in the totalizing
framework of an atheistic regime. Thus we are forced to ask
a *historical* question and to bring further sociological principles into play which have to do with the redeployment by
the new regime of an archaic inertia. This means that churches
do not necessarily cease to be churches when their historical
circumstances change, precisely because there are social
forces which reproduce for many generations an essential
churchly character. The church still does not exhibit tension
with the atheistic environment, or challenge the distribution
of power, and it accepts one crucial element from the old
system of mutually supportive relations, i.e., state influence
on ecclesiastical leadership.

We have here a fascinating set of highly complex sociological rules about what is possible and likely with regard to
the structure of appointment in a situation like the U.S.S.R.,
and what range of options the ecclesiastical elite has open to
it. We also have rules which stress the continuity of particular patterns over time, and which suggest why one aspect of
a preexisting pattern may be retained while others are
dropped. Such illustrations of the inertial thrust of the past
into the present, which we can rephrase as the reproductive

power of culture, especially religious culture, make us ask just how important are certain other elements which might be reasonably included in the definition of church, such as being the majority or the largest single group in a given area.

All these sociological rules and all these sociological insights about reproductive inertias arise directly from an exploration of the dialectic between exceptions and the kind of definition which contains co-relations. That is not to say, of course, that one could not have arrived at this corpus of sociological rules and this emphasis on history and on histori-cal inertias from some other angle or from a different point of departure. As I suggested initially, you can arrive at the same *terminus ad quem* from a variety of starting points, though not from *any* starting point. (It may be, of course, that an approach which plays off exceptions against definitions avoids most of the matters complained about by Stark and Bainbridge.)

Perhaps I could develop the glancing references made in the above discussion to such plausible characteristics of a church as constituting a majority and being sympathetically regarded by the elite. It seems that a church may remain the same in its essential character, indeed in almost every respect, whether or not it is in a majority, whether or not the elite is sympathetic. This is in spite of the fact that such qualities belong to a churchly character, and reinforce it, and in a quite crucial way give rise to that character in the first place. (What determined sociological character initially may be shed and yet that character be retained.) The Russian case seems clear enough. The Russian Orthodox Church is not in the majority, and in some areas never has been, and the elite is far from sympathetic. The Irish case points in the same direction. The Roman Catholic Church in Ireland was out of alignment with the English elite up to 1922, but its character was the same before and after that date. The Roman Catholic Church is a minority in Northern Ireland but it is exactly the same church, ecclesiastically and sociologically, north or south of the border. In Northern Ireland it is certainly in tension with its environment, which happens to consist largely of English Anglicans and Calvinistic Scots, but it is *not* a sect.

Being in Tension

None of the above observations has made it inappropriate to include the reference to the mutual support of ecclesiastical and social elites in the definition. Nor have these observations made it *irrelevant*, for example, to think of churches in relation to majorities in given societies. What these observations have made clear is the particular way these "normal," and perhaps original, aspects of churchliness may be absent without affecting churchly character. Moreover, these observations have directed attention to what exactly is meant by "being in tension" with the environment, since the concept of tension is so crucial to Stark and Bainbridge in distinguishing churches from both sects and cults.

"Being in tension" with the environment is not an unambiguous attribute. Yet it is the point of departure for Stark and Bainbridge when they come to distinguishing churches from sects and cults, and I may say that I agree with their broad emphasis. But this state of tension needs now to be unpacked. The Roman Catholic Church in Northern Ireland may be "in tension" with the environment, but that is because that environment comprises two other churches, with the same kind of links with ethnic groups which the Roman Church itself possesses. The media men may talk about "sectarianism" in Northern Ireland but the sociological essence of the problem arises precisely because there are three distinct *churches* and three ethnic groups in a narrow space, with the spirals of mutual segregation which that brings about in two large towns, Belfast and Londonderry. *All* these churches, when taken separately, are minorities, just as *all* the religious groups in Lebanon are, taken separately, minorities. And what follows is not that the Roman, Presbyterian and Anglican bodies are not true churches, for they each function as such in relation to their respective communities, and to the areas where their strength is maximally concentrated. What follows is a whole set of sociological rules and relations which are operative in such places as Northern Ireland and Lebanon where the environmental tension is of this *particular* kind. What happens, that is to say, where the tension with the environment is precisely *not* sectarian but arises because rival churches have jostling, partly overlapping, boundaries within a single small political unit?

Obviously, this is not the only kind of tension. The religious bodies of North and Central Wales are in tension with the wider society of Wales as a whole and also with England because they have certain moral priorities with respect to Sunday closing. These link in with the issue of the Welsh language to provide symbols of identity over against cosmopolitan and secular influences. The tension with the wider environment is very strong, precisely because the identification of the religious bodies with the *local* environment is so close. I would be reluctant to call the various Calvinistic bodies of North and Central Wales sects. Indeed, I would revert to the category of denomination, which was omitted from the article of Stark and Bainbridge, and constitutes another grouping of characteristics to be pondered over, in between sects and cults on the one hand, and churches on the other. Welsh religious bodies are, in fact, classical denominations, which compete with each other in more or less friendly rivalry. Because they are concentrated in a particular area under secular, cosmopolitan threat, they also manage to fulfill certain symbolic roles of a churchly kind, e.g., the relation of a church and a people, a church and a territory. But they are not churches. On the other hand, their small size, taken in itself, and the special kind of tension with the wider environment which they exhibit, do not make them sectarian. The tension arises not out of their own repudiation of the culture in which they live and move, nor does it arise out of any serious world-rejecting intransigence central to their viewpoint. They are, taken in themselves, neither so intransigent nor morally so peculiar as to arouse intense spirals of mutual repulsion. It just so happens that in the historical contingent situation of North and Central Wales, their mild idiosyncracies can be taken up into wider patterns of cultural defense and local symbolism.

And where does *this* lead? Well, I've already touched on the category of denomination, which I would say has enough *more or less* linked characteristics to be considered separately. However, I haven't space to go into that here, and in any case, I did so in 1962 in the *British Journal of Sociology*[4] in a discussion which was mentioned in the excellent article by Benton Johnson to which Stark and Bainbridge very properly refer. Where it does lead, so far as the main issue is concerned, is toward two questions.

One is that we have to ask precisely what *kind* of tension with society is crucial when we are trying either to delineate sects, or for that matter, to characterize the particular variety of cult which Stark and Bainbridge describe as a cult *movement*, rather than a cultic *audience*, or a cultic *form of therapy*. The other question is whether we may use a particular kind of tension, not merely as a useful starting point which we happen to have lighted on, but as a genuine empirical *hub* from which other elements tend to flow and radiate.

Actually, I repeat, I am in agreement with Stark and Bainbridge in that the degree of tension with society is of great importance. I am inclined to believe that somewhere within that concept there is a certain *kind* of tension which provides a hub from which other empirical correlates radiate. In my book on *Pacifism* published in 1965, I tended to identify that hub for the sect in the rejection and inversion of the orderings and priorities of the social order and social hierarchy taken as a whole, together with a refusal of the apparatus of coercion and legitimized violence.[5] That is a strong type of definition, framed for a purpose, but it would fit in with the emphasis and direction of the Stark and Bainbridge article.

What I still do not see, however, is why we should reject concepts based on more or less linked phenomena, and not use the exceptions to explore and unearth a wider and wider net of sociological rules in the manner I tried to indicate earlier. That dialectic of definition and exception can be very fruitful. I also do not see why the delineation of sub-types needs to be set aside quite so vigorously as do Stark and Bainbridge. The denomination remains a useful concept. Moreover, I notice strong parallels between the sub-types of cult devised by Stark and Bainbridge and some of the categories of sect earlier devised by Bryan Wilson in *The American Sociological Review.*[6] Admittedly, sub-types are sometimes added to sub-types with needless disregard for the elegant parsimony recommended and exemplified by Stark and Bainbridge. Yet the Wilson types did yield a wide net of observations about etiology, provenance, dynamics and sect life-history, which I think gave them a strong empirical grounding. I submit that one can be too parsimonious.

Cults and Correlates

In the second main section of my critical comment, I wish to focus more directly to the category of "cult" as formulated by Stark and Bainbridge, though inevitably some of the same general issues arise. Of course, what I have argued so far with respect to the principles governing the use of "church" applies to the use of "cult." Just as I am inclined to put together several "correlates" in a preliminary, heuristic definition of "church," so I am inclined to link such correlates in a definition of "cult." However, once I attempt such a definition and place it alongside that utilized by Stark and Bainbridge, certain other theoretical issues arise of considerable importance and interest. The very fact that such issues arise in this way might be thought sufficient justification for playing off the type of "linked" definition which I employ against the single variable approach adopted by Stark and Bainbridge. A consideration of different heuristic devices for organizing definitional "grips" in reality often reveals fresh problems about that reality.

I must begin then by referring back to the kind of definition of "cult" I have been wont to deploy in the past. Readers will note that it differs from the definition utilized by Stark and Bainbridge. My view of cult takes off from a cultic individualism which has separated itself from the corporate emphasis of all Christian bodies, even the denominations, whereas Stark and Bainbridge take off from the phenomenon of foreignness, novelty and tension. (Actually, it occurs to me that the Stark and Bainbridge formulation is not so innocent of "correlates" as they would ideally wish. Being foreign, new and "oppositional" are presumably postulated correlates. But let that be. From my point of view *ça ne fait rien.*) My own formulation of the concept of cult relates quite closely to the notion of "the self religions":

> The fundamental criterion of the cult is therefore individualism. It is neither a worshipping community, like church, order and denomination, nor is it the closely-knit separated band of the elect. The highest level of interpersonal action is a "parallelism of spontaneities", more particularly of the kind involved in the common pursuit of psychological techniques or therapeutic discussion. The most characteristic form of face-to-face relationship is that of teacher (or *guru*) towards initiate, although in many cases communication is restricted to correspondence and the circulation of books. Thus a high degree of centralized organization may be associated with a very low degree of personal contact. The content of correspondence is more likely to be psychological advice than devotional reading.
>
> However, individualism has many manifestations and

the cult normally bifurcates in two broad directions. These need to be analyzed because they are relevant to the way in which members of this type of group react to war. The first kind of cult lacks the mystical strain just discussed and is largely concerned with enabling the individual to fulfill the norms of his particular environment, by making him more self-assured, by increasing his intellectual power and by equipping him with manipulative techniques. It therefore meets the condition of those people who do not know how to maximize their opportunities.

The range of such groups will clearly vary from Pelmanism at one extreme, which is highly specific and almost totally manipulative, to Scientology, which is not merely manipulative but also provides an apparatus of confession and interrogation derived from modern psychology, police methods, and the practice of the Catholic Church. Also within this range lie those organizations, of which Christian Science is the best known, which offer release from bodily ills through a correct metaphysical and psychological approach. Quite plainly whether the main emphasis is on social manipulation or on psychological and bodily health, *no norms will be generated which set the member in conflict with society.* Thus when confronted by the challenge of war the member will react simply in conformity with social demands. His religion or psychological system will now assist him to adjust in his new role as soldier.

However, the second kind of cult is generally concerned with a programme of self-mastery and cultivation in terms of a condition of personal grace which may differ radically from the ideal of the wider society. While the manipulative type just discussed may be expected to have more appeal for the commercial middle class, the type based on mastery in terms of a condition of personal grace may rather appeal to professionals and academics.[7]

I have inserted an emphasis, not in the original text, with respect to the phrase, "no norms will be generated which set the member in conflict with society." That remains my position, since the aim of the manipulative type of cult is expressly to assist social performance, but I must add that some of the cult techniques may arouse opposition or criticism, such as occurred in relation to Scientology, thereby placing the cult practitioner willy-nilly in conflict with the wider society.

This definition, when placed alongside the Stark and Bainbridge formulation, will be seen to bring into focus the theoretical issues mentioned above and further illustrated below. They related to foreignness and novelty, as stressed by Stark and Bainbridge, and they bear on the extent to which religious bodies retain certain basic characteristics over time and over cultural spaces and frontiers. Of course, to cross a cultural frontier or to move into a new historical phase must make some difference, but the juxtaposition of definitions poses the question of just *how* great the difference is. Moreover, precisely this question of continuity of sociological character over cultural space and time arose earlier in pursuing the dialectic between the definition of church and the variations in empirical reality. This underlines its theoretical importance.

Alien and Exotic

Let me take the foreignness of cults as postulated by Stark and Bainbridge. Of course, this has one advantage, which is its adoption by the media. Moreover, there is no doubt that being foreign usually makes some difference, though Nicheron Shoshu manages to have many more members in Britain than the Unification Church, without any of the conflict experienced by "Moonies." All the same, a theoretical focus on the fact of "foreignness" obscures the very different character of varied importations and removes the continuity of social character which so often survives the crossing of frontiers. It places all emphasis on "a sea change into something rich and strange."

The point can be illustrated by reference to the importation of Roman Catholicism into seventeenth-century Japan. There is no doubt that after an initial period of peaceful co-existence, the Catholic Church was in acute and painful

tension with the wider society. However, that was not because it had adopted some sectarian rejection of "the world,"
but for various political and strategic reasons which made it
appear a potential rival church. It retained all the churchly
characteristics evolved in its original European habitat. Indeed,
it is arguable that the tension arose, at least in part, precisely because churchly ambitions were inherited from Europe.

To turn the point around a bit, I do not see that a
religious body can be designated a cult by reason of "tension"
as such, whether or not that tension derives from the fact of
novelty and foreign importation. The Roman Church in South
Africa is in tension with the wider society, or more precisely, the Afrikaaner ethos and the government, because it
retains the universalistic scope of a church and will not bow
to local criteria of ethnicity. It has no long term quarrel with
mundane society or with the institutions of mundane society, such as are found in classic Christian sectarianism. With
a change of government or governmental policy, tension
might be eased or eliminated. To say this is, once again, to
repeat points made earlier both about continuity of social
character and about the highly contingent nature of certain
kinds of tension associated with ethnic conflict and governmental policy. The Roman Catholic Church approves of secular government as such, and conflicts from time to time with
particular governments, e.g., in the U.S.S.R., whereas
Jehovah's Witnesses seek an entirely new kind of gover-
nance and therefore run across *all* governments, e.g., in the
U.S.S.R. But it does not follow that where the Catholic
Church and the Jehovah's Witnesses are jointly in tension
with the wider society they share a common sociological
character. The Catholics in Lithuania are churchly, and the
Jehovah's Witnesses in Siberia are sectarian.

Once more, the *kind* of tension is pretty crucial, and the
more one looks at the criterion of tension deployed by Stark
and Bainbridge, the more it fragments. Admittedly, most
sociologists of religion have, from time to time, appealed to

the notion of tension without unpacking the myriad forms which it assumes. All the same, the kinds of tension are, in fact, so varied that it is difficult to see how they can be placed along a continuum of *degrees* of tension. Even the Church of England, which heaven and everyone else knows is a *church*, can get in tension with its environment. The General Synod recently voted against the government's nationality bill by 180 to 1. It was, however, an odd kind of tension. The vote went against the government certainly, and I suspect it also defied majority opinion, especially in the working class. But, on the other hand, it was in conformity with the presuppositions of the left-liberal upper middle class. Nothing follows from the vote with respect to the churchly character of the Church of England. What follows is that we have to examine very carefully what we mean by "tension" and "the status quo."

There is one further point to be made. It seems to me that one has to be cautious about the way Stark and Bainbridge distinguish respectively between sects and cults, by whether or not they split off from parent bodies or emerge *sui generis* by spontaneous generation and *innovation*. Of course, the dynamics of schism within an existing body are different from the dynamics whereby a religious body emerges *de novo*. But it does not follow that this difference can immediately be linked to restoration of the old in the one case, and innovation in the other. Schism is notoriously innovative, as the case of the Old Believers illustrates, and religious orders, which are a sort of schism without explicit break, restore and innovate simultaneously. Michael Hill, in his book *The Religious Order*, speaks of a "Revolution by Tradition" and it is a process which occurs outside the particular context he had in mind.[8] After all, restorations work by *creatively imagining* the past, not by reproducing it.

In sum, I am unhappy with characterizations of "cult" which depend on novelty, on high tension with the environment, e.g., a general "oppositional" character, and on foreignness. Insofar as I discern a "foreign" element in the cult, it arises not by reason of importation across frontiers, but because the cultic emphasis on the individual is somewhat askew the corporate nature of all the classic manifestations of the Christian tradition. The "self religions" may or may not be imported, but they arise under modern conditions which eat into and corrode traditional corporateness. They should be distinguished from sects, not by their capacity to innovate since sects are highly innovative, but by their congruence with a nascent modern individualism. Sects, like churches, retain the group-oriented character of Christianity, whereas cults move outside the Christian ambit. No doubt, part of the argument is simply a matter of how we decide to use words, but quite considerable theoretical issues hang on whether we emphasize the individual-corporate continuum or the foreign-indigenous continuum, and also on whether it is empirically plausible to distinguish sects and cults by their rejection or promotion of innovation.

NOTES

1 Rodney Stark and William Bainbridge, "Of Churches, Sects, and Cults: Preliminary Concepts for a Theory of Religious Movements," *Journal for the Scientific Study of Religion*, 18, no. 2 (1979): 117-31.
2 Benton Johnson, "On Church and Sect," *American Sociological Review*, 28, no. 4 (August 1963): 539-49.
3 Stark and Bainbridge, p. 121.
4 David A. Martin, "The Denomination," *British Journal of Sociology*, 13, no. 1 (March 1962): 1-14.
5 David A. Martin, *Pacifism: An Historical and Sociological Study* (London: Routledge & Kegan Paul, 1965).
6 Bryan R. Wilson, "An Analysis of Sect Development," *American Sociological Review*, 24, no. 1 (February 1959): 3-15.
7 Martin, *Pacifism*, pp. 194-95.
8 Michael Hill, *The Religious Order* (London: Heinemann, 1975).

Part II:
Metaphysical Alternatives

Spiritual Frontiers Fellowship

Melinda Bollar Wagner

The bulk of the literature on alternative religious movements leaves the impression that these groups are new,
exist mainly in California, and attract disaffected youth. The
function most often ascribed to these groups is that they
provide their youthful adherents with a sense of "community"
which they find otherwise missing in their lives. These
impressions have been empirically verified for a portion of
the "new religions." But there is another type of religious
movement which has been largely ignored by social scientists.
One of these is the Spiritual Frontiers Fellowship which is
the subject of this study.

Certain characteristics of this "metaphysical" religious
movement differentiate it from the better known cults and
denominations. It exists mainly in the midwestern United
States, attracts middle-class, middle-aged people, and is not
the recent product of an alienated generation. This movement does not provide a sense of "community" for its
followers. Instead, it offers its members a flexible "meaning"
in a flexible world. Like other metaphysical groups, the
Spiritual Frontiers Fellowship encourages individual spiritual growth, but it is unique among them in its desire to
interest leaders of orthodox churches in psychic phenomena
and spiritual healing.

Metaphysics and the Occult

The Spiritual Frontiers Fellowship has been catego-
rized by J. Stillson Judah as part of the American "metaphysical movement," which also includes Christian Science,
Theosophy, Spiritualism, the Astara Foundation, the Unity
School of Christianity, the Association for Research and
Enlightenment, and several New Thought groups.[1] These
groups are not affiliated in a formal organization, but they
all subscribe to the view that metaphysics is a "practical

religious philosophy." They are interested in relating spiritual and psychic phenomena to everyday life. The earlier
metaphysical groups in America were established in the
latter part of the nineteenth century and continued to multi-
ply, with more than half of them founded since 1950.

The Fellowship, which now has a membership of about
five thousand, dates its beginning to Evanston, Illinois, in
1956. The original founders were predominantly Protestant
midwesterners who were religious leaders and laymen. As
a participant observer at the local, regional, and national
organizational levels during the course of fifteen months
(from September, 1974 to January, 1976), I was frequently
told of the individualistic character of the metaphysical
movement: its primary goal is to encourage and promote
the spiritual growth of each member. This is perceived as a
process of becoming increasingly aware of one's "divine"
inner self. Through this ongoing process the members discover the "meaning" of their own human existence.

The leader of a small local Study Group, whose weekly
meetings I observed for its one-year life, put the question to
the members: "What has spiritual growth meant to you?"
One response was given by "Grace," a widow in her fifties,
who was preparing to retire from her job as a stenographer:

> In 1955 I had a tragedy in my life. At that time, I decided
> there had to be something more to life beyond just eating,
> sleeping, and working. I began searching. We started a heal-
> ing class at church, where we read all the parts of the Bible
> having to do with healing. Then I went into Silva Mind
> Control, Transcendental Meditation, and other classes. But
> never till now did I feel that I'd found it.

Spiritual growth was seen as achieving a new identity
by "Sara," a 33-year-old homemaker and mother of one,
who said it was a matter of "learning about my inner self. In
me there's been an evolutionary change—a complete change
from ten years ago to the present. It's like a new life. If I find
myself in any kind of trouble, I turn myself to God, just tune

myself into God. And I just vibrate from my feet right up to the top of my head." The "it" Grace has found, and the "new life" which allows Sara to accept herself, are examples of renewed and improved "identity." In these cases, the identifying reference point is an "inner self." Life now has meaning for these women because they have solved, or are on the way to solving, the problem of identity.

Individuals in complex societies seem especially troubled by "meaninglessness" and have devised all sorts of ways of combatting it.[2] Two trends in contemporary American society could be said to dissolve meaning. One of these is societal "differentiation," the institutional specialization and role diversification which have been accentuated by industrialization. Bellah sees modern existence as an almost "infinite possibility thing" where we suffer from what Toffler called "overchoice."[3] The second trend is the "rationalization" of all the potential and diversified choices. The potential reference points through which we might find meaning are discursive and rational. They are empirical and thus subject to rapid change. It is the nondiscursive symbol (such as God) which best serves as a referent for establishing identity, for it is not empirical; it cannot be verified, but neither can it be falsified. These two trends—differentiation, which leads to autonomy in the choice of meaning, and an overemphasis on the discursive, which renders some potential meaning-givers useless—have helped make the identity search a major American activity.

The search for meaning in American society takes many forms, not all of which are "religious." The women's liberation movement, or conservation groups like the Sierra Club, may provide identity. Natural foods, art, travel, surfing, body-building, or motorcycle clubs can be used as referents for establishing identity. But it cannot be denied that interest in things spiritual, "occult," and "metaphysical" is high. The extent of this interest has been well-documented.[4] Yet not all persons who are interested in the occult build their meaning around it. Truzzi said that most "play" with the occult, but a "small but significant minority" uses its beliefs and principles in a "search for new sacred elements."[5] This "small but significant minority" uses occult and metaphysical ideas and practices in a way which can be defined as religious in Geertz's terms. For Geertz, religion is "a system of symbols which acts to establish powerful, pervasive, and long-lasting moods and motivations in men, by formulating conceptions of a general order of existence, and clothing those conceptions with such an aura of factuality that the moods and motivations seem uniquely realistic."[6] That is, religion—whatever ideas and symbols a person uses as "religion"—provides answers to the questions posed by the existence of life and death, and "good" and "evil."

The new movements which are "religious" in these terms are themselves quite diverse, and make various responses to the differentiated and discursive nature of American culture. Spiritual Frontiers Fellowship's response is to maintain a loosely-knit "Occult Establishment." This is a term invented by Martin Marty to distinguish groups like the Fellowship from others that belong in the "Occult Underground," where meaning is found in close communion with a guru or charismatic leader. The devotees of Hare Krishna and Meher Baba tend to reside in small communes, ashrams or temples, where they obey a set of strict norms organizing all aspects of their daily lives. Choices are minimal and are highly institutionalized, demanding a spiritual conformity that runs counter to the surrounding choice-filled and materialistic culture.

The Spiritual Frontiers Fellowship, however, resembles Marty's occult establishment in that it is neither countercultural nor communitarian.[7] None of SFF's three organizational levels could be said to be "communal" in orientation. There are approximately 330 local study groups, each meeting once weekly, usually for a year, with eight to twelve people to discuss such topics as astrology, life after death, psychic healing, reincarnation, and spirit communication. At the regional level there are seventy-three groups in thirty-five states, most of which schedule an invited speaker for their monthly meetings. Finally, there is a national office located in Independence, Missouri, to which members pay their annual dues.

The Expression of Autonomy

Unlike the new communal religious movements, Spiritual Frontiers Fellowship deliberately attempts to legitimate the autonomy of its members, and even deifies the independent and individual "self." The basic philosophy is that all persons must find their own path to truth. SFF presents a variety of beliefs and viewpoints from which its members may select. Individuals are free to fashion their own meaning from this array, accepting some concepts and rejecting others. "The only essentials are loyalty to the truth as one perceives it, and willingness to venture out in obedience to it."[8] A national leader spoke of the "free marketplace of ideas." Study Group leaders are advised that each member should feel free to work out a personal interpretation of psychic phenomena. As one member remarked, "the nice thing about metaphysics is that you can look at these things with an open mind, believe what you want to believe and take the best from each one of them."

A symbol of the results of shopping at the free marketplace of ideas was displayed in the home of the leader of the Study Group which I observed for a year. Jenny's living room was the setting for our weekly meetings. On one wall were two pictures of Christ, one with a peaceful expression, the other pained, bearing a crown of thorns and drops of blood. On another wall were a large picture of the many-armed Hindu god, Shiva, and a small framed round photograph of the Roman Catholic stigmatic, Padre Pio. A table between two chairs had the shape of an elephant with an Indian howdah on its back. In the corner stood a three-foot high black Buddha, holding a candle in one outstretched hand. Arranged on the fireplace mantle were candles, a Confucius figurine, a bronze bust of an American Indian, a figure of a tree, a Madonna statuette, and a crystal ball. Jenny had drawn on all the belief systems symbolized in the room, and had formulated her own belief system.

The only valid criterion recognized by Spiritual Frontiers for establishing one's own truth is personal experience. A student is admonished not to "let others lead you," but rather to "listen to God. Meditate and let God show you." The way to "test" or discern truth is by intuitive religious experience.[9] A message or insight received while "meditating and letting God show you" would serve as an experience capable of validating truth. It would be seen as an "experimental demonstration" of this truth, as would a message received in a dream, or during hypnosis. Experience in the use of psychic powers could also be used to verify beliefs. The development of one's own psychic abilities "proves" the existence of these abilities. If a person can "do" psychometry (receiving messages about a person by holding an object which belongs to him) or if one has "seen" things clairvoyantly, then these phenomena must exist. The amelioration of health conditions is used to "prove" spiritual healing. Recovering from an illness is an experience capable of validating the efficacy of healing. The closer and more personal the healing is, the greater is its "proof" value. Hearing a report of healing is not as convincing as witnessing a healing in one's own family. The most compelling of proof is being healed oneself.

The rationale for the individual's ability to accept and interpret truth is in the Fellowship's two central beliefs: first, that "God is within" and second, that direct and ongoing communication with God is possible. In other words, every human being is thought to harbor an inner spark of divinity.[10] Communication with the God within is achieved through prayer and meditation. "Prayer is talking to God, or one's divine inner self. Meditation is listening to God." The rituals of solitary prayer and meditation are particularly well-suited to a religious philosophy which emphasizes individualism. No ritual space is necessary; neither is ritual paraphernalia, nor a ritual practitioner. All you need is your own body, mind, and soul, as the SFF members would say.

The principles of individual exegesis and personal experience as the authority for truth indicate that the Fellowship is not dogmatic in the presentation of its beliefs, but considers itself "creedless," as do the other groups in the American metaphysical movement.[11] Arthur Ford, one of the founders of Spiritual Frontiers Fellowship, described what the group "really stands for" when he extolled "free inquiry, free thinking, free investigation, and the religion based upon experience rather than dogma."[12] The conviction that the group has no dogma is so strong that this conviction itself almost becomes a dogma. The literature of the Fellowship and the presentations of speakers at its functions are replete with caveats that "what I say is not necessarily true for you."

Individualistic Structure

The principles of individual exegesis and internal authority are well served by the non-hierarchical, autonomous and anti-authoritarian nature of the Fellowship's structure. Since the individuals are their own theologians, as well as their own priests, the very notion of membership must remain loose and decentralized. Membership in Spiritual Frontiers Fellowship does not preclude membership in other spiritual organizations. The primary reason exclusive membership is not required is that it would be disconsant with a philosophy that the individuals are their own authority for truth. If the members internalize the concept that they must find their own path to truth, and that this can be found in many sources, they are likely to feel that the more groups they participate in, the better. There is evidence that mem-

bership in several organizations, either simultaneously or
serially, is characteristic of adherents to the metaphysical
movements.[13] A brochure advertising one of the Fellowship's
week-long retreats described a workshop leader as a prominent architect who is a member of the Executive Council
and a long-time student of the paranormal. "He is a member
of the Institute of Noetic Sciences, the Association for Research and Enlightenment, Fellowship of Spiritual Understanding, ESP Associates, and the Academy of Psychology
and Medicine."

Participation in several groups simultaneously is facilitated by the varying degrees of commitment commonly
allowed in metaphysical groups.[14] A person's commitments
can be parcelled out as he or she sees fit, and can accommo-
date individual needs. Solitary study and meditation is one
form, gregarious fellowship another. One can become a
dependent follower, or a depended-upon psychic professional.
Within the Fellowship, members may participate in any or
all of the three organizational levels, local, regional, or
national, or in any combination of these. Official membership can be obtained only through the National Office in
Independence, but national membership is not required for
participation in regional activities, or in study groups. The
regional groups are autonomous with regard to programming,
and are financially self-supporting. Study groups are likewise autonomous and are advised by the National Office
that they should allow "maximum inner growth with mini-
mum outer organization."[15]

Spiritual Frontiers Fellowship's anti-authoritarian style
of leadership reflects and supports its individualistic stance.
There is no recognized charismatic leader at the national
level, and the Fellowship has taken steps to avoid the ascen-
dancy of any guru. Two of the original founders, who are
active participants, enjoy a degree of respect, but not
reverence. The presidency is an elective office, with short
tenure. According to former president Althouse, "limiting

the tenure of the president to two two-year terms helps to keep SFF from being identified as any one person's 'thing.' SFF has never been a 'one-person show.' "[16] At the area level the directing role is shared by a chairperson and a steering committee, and at the local level the study group is guided by a "facilitator," or "moderator." If there is a sense of "community," it centers on the personality of the local study group leaders, most of whom are women. While the study group moderator is meant to be a non-authoritarian "facilitator," she tends to be a persuasive charismatic person who is thought to have more highly developed charisms, or gifts of the spirit, than the other members.

In relation to the larger organization, however, study group leaders demonstrated their independence in 1975 when the National Office tried to impose membership quotas and legislated that at least three-fourths of any local group must pay national dues. Local leaders opposed this quota rule, and the dissatisfaction was sufficiently widespread to cause the national leadership to revise it.

Autonomy and Fellowship

Unlike the close-knit communes of the so-called "occult underground" groups, Spiritual Frontiers Fellowship does not build a permanent community in which one is sheltered from industrialized society's specialized, unemotional, and fragmenting roles. The Fellowship does try, however, to alleviate the sense of separation from others by "seeking to provide a comfortable climate for sharing and discussing experiences of nonphysical reality." Members meet face-to-face weekly in study groups (but usually for just one year), monthly at area meetings, and occasionally at retreats conducted for a weekend or a full week.

A "mail-order fellowship" fostered by correspondence from the national organization may serve to alleviate a feeling of separateness by confirming that there are others, around the country, who share the reader's metaphysical interests. Area meetings and retreats provide opportunities for "fellowship" where group rituals, like healing services and group meditations, may be performed. But the "fellowship" attained through these contacts is sporadic, casual, and short-lived. It is the local study group that provides the best opportunity for developing fellowship.

The metaphysical study group, with its weekly meetings, is characterized by close but temporary primary relationships, and the leader exemplifies the kind of facilitator that Charles Fair calls a "listener-helper."[17] Jenny, the leader of the study group I observed, often remarked that in the old days, neighbors were friends who talked out their problems over the back fence. "Neighbors aren't close anymore, and you don't talk across the back fence. Today people can go to a psychiatrist; but they're expensive. So, people come to groups like this, and to me." Despite the official metaphysical stance against dependent followers and strong leaders, the group I observed did revolve around Jenny.

The individual members of Jenny's study group drove from a fifty-mile radius to attend the weekly meetings; most were not neighbors and had no contact between meetings. In Parsons' terminology, the members' roles were largely "instrumental" rather than "expressive." The meetings were not an end in themselves, but a means of achieving spiritual growth. The role of study group member is a specific one, characterized by partial involvement with other members, rather than the total involvement associated with expressive roles. Unlike the "ideal type" instrumental role, however, the role of study group member did lead to affective relationships. There was much talk in the group of "rapport" and "harmony." The members often said "we all help each other." A portion of each meeting was devoted to a "sharing of psychic and spiritual experiences" which was essentially a discussion of personal problems. Any sort of therapy or mutual-help group could have provided this kind of sharing. But the Study Group was joined in ways these other groups could not have been—through rituals, psychic means of maintaining contact, and a mythos which joined members together in past reincarnations.

Group rituals served as a basis for shared experiences. Each group meeting ended with a "healing circle" during which all members stood holding hands. Sometimes in this circle, energy was thought to be passed from one person to the next, around the circle, so that eventually everyone's energy had passed through everyone else. Time was always set aside in the meetings for a group meditation. Everyone meditated on the same subject, and the experiences and insights gained in meditation were shared with the group. Members were drawn closer together if they had similar experiences during meditation. Jenny said if she "tuned in on it" she could "go with" other persons in meditation, and see what they were seeing, or be where they were. Even while they were physically distant, the study group members were expected to meditate daily so that they could "mentally visualize the face of each group member and send them a good thought or a prayer. This enables the group to get in tune and helps develop rapport."[18] "Astral travel" or "out-of-body experiences" were discussed as ways of maintaining contact with group members when physically separated from them.

The concept of reincarnation was also a means of enhancing group cohesion. During the year of my field experience with the Study Group, a series of reincarnation accounts were woven which joined group members together in prior lives, because "you don't come together in a group as close as this unless you have been together before." In one instance the leader, Jenny, and several other members had been nuns in a convent in France in the eighteenth century. Jenny had been the Mother Superior, and while in the convent, she raised one of the other group members who had been orphaned in this prior life. Such common experiences in their past lives sanctified their relationships,

making of them something different from the ordinary relationships encountered in the workaday world. Reincarnation gave the Study Group a note of perpetuity it would not
have otherwise had. The members had been together before;
perhaps they would be again.

Self-Realization Through Spiritual Growth

While providing arenas for "fellowship" is a concern
for SFF, fostering group identity is not its ultimate goal. The
main goal of the highly individualistic metaphysical groups
is the encouragement of individual spiritual growth, or self-
realization. For all their individualism and emphasis on the
self, however, the metaphysicians are not completely human-
centered. They have left the community out of their religious equation, but they have not omitted God. For the self
they are seeking to know is the *divine* inner self. This
monistic view of man and God is common to Eastern
philosophies, but is, as the metaphysical groups recognize,
opposed to Judeo-Christian dualism. Historians of the metaphysical movements have traced the Western roots of their
monism back to the Platonic sense of the "whole of being,"
through the gnostics, to the New England Transcendentalists.[19]
According to Metaphysical philosophy, great spiritual teachers such as Jesus, Buddha, and Muhammad had the same
modicum of divinity every person has, but they were more
aware of their divinity than most.

A metaphorical relationship with the divine lies at the
base of the identity—or self-realization—gained through
spiritual growth. The use of metaphor ameliorates the separation of humans from their world which van Baal theorized
is a result of man's ability to express his experiences by
means of symbols.[20] Symbolizing is objectifying. Symbolizing makes subjects of us all as we make objects of all that we
talk or think about. By the use of metaphor, we can objectify
ourselves. That is, the subject takes the point of view of "the
other" at the object end of the copula. The process of

identification involves moving "from the preoccupation with the predicate back across the copula to an understanding of the subject and its difference" from the object. "Metaphors move us, and their aptness lies in their power to change our moods, our sense of situation."[21]

The metaphorical relationship with the divine found in SFF can be expressed as:

God is my inner self,
My higher self is God,
I am God, or
I am

The metaphor is used two ways. In the first instance, "God" is the subject. God is "located" in "my inner self." I have derived this metaphor from a leader's insistence that "God is within...God is in here (in the heart), within us." By accepting the "God is my inner-self" metaphor, the metaphysical student is accepting the belief that God dwells within, and is readily available to meet individual needs for communication with the divine. In the second metaphor, "My higher self is God" or "I am God," "my higher self" or "I" is the subject. This metaphor establishes the divinity of one's own inner self. I have derived this metaphor from SFF's concept that each person has a spark of divinity. As the metaphysicians see it, seeking the kingdom of heaven within should ultimately lead to a sense of identification with God and the universe, called "the I am" or "at-one-ment." Jenny describes it as "at-one-ment" because when it is achieved the aspirant feels "at one" with God, the universe, and all humanity, while experiencing internal "wholeness."

Spiritual growth and all its advantages—inner peace, meaningfulness, prosperity, happiness—derive from an increasing awareness of the God within. In the metaphysical movements, "man is God, or more conservatively, becomes ever more like him."[22] Achieving this sense of wholeness does not require that a person retire from society, to sit in the lotus position in some distant ashram. In fact, one woman (a cashier) reported that she meditated at lunchtime in the rest room at K-Mart. She said that this interval of meditation helped her to be in a good mood when she dealt with customers in the afternoon. In worldly and pragmatic terms SFF leader Hayes remarks, "Spiritual growth is a process of becoming a better person on the physical level through your relationships with other people."[23]

Spiritual growth is a satisfactory means of establishing self-identity because the "God within" is a spiritual symbol and, therefore, meets the criterion for an unempirical, unfalsifiable center for one's being. Spiritual growth depends on the nondiscursive ritual of meditation, a religious experience which provides a sense of wholeness—a union of symboling subject and symbolized object, or "self" and "other." Spiritual growth is thought to result in many practical benefits, among them the possibility of "evolution" from an inchoate and fragmented identity to a whole and harmonious one, from negative to positive attitudes and relationships in everyday life experiences, from a less to a more healthy physical state, from an unenlightened position alongside the "masses of humanity" to an enlightened position among the metaphysically aware, and from a lower to a higher level of psychic ability.

Scientific Religious Philosophy

The founders of the Spiritual Frontiers Fellowship felt that modern society places too much emphasis on the material or physical aspects of life, and depends too heavily on discursive symbols and rational modes of learning and understanding. The response to this misplaced emphasis is to encourage interest in the spiritual side of life and to favor intuitive, experiential modes of communication. Yet on the other hand, the Fellowship and the other metaphysical groups consider metaphysics a *scientific* religious philosophy.[24] SFF is both a spiritual reaction against a culture it considers too "material," and an expression of the need to be "scientific" in today's world.

Spiritual Frontiers accuses the mainline churches of neglecting emotion and mysticism and of becoming too "rationalistic."[25] The movement's epistemology is nondiscursive, and favors experiential, intuitive modes of knowing and communicating. Personal experience is the recognized criterion for truth, and is preferred over other methods of learning, such as reading or listening to a lecture. One leader drew the distinction between knowledge and wisdom with the remark that "knowledge is gained by reading and listening. Wisdom is gained by meditating and letting God show you."

The emphasis on the "spiritual side of life" was also manifested in spiritual explanations for problems discussed within the Study Group. Much of what the Study Group did was to deal with members' quotidian problems. But the manner in which they were treated differed from that of any kind of psychologically oriented self-help group. Problems were spiritually explained and spiritually solved. For example, a man in the Study Group was having trouble with his boss. The explanation was that he and his boss had been together in a past life when they had also had a troubled relationship. The solution for this difficulty was to put the relationship in the "Pure White Light of the Christ." Metaphysicians also put faith in the power of thought and the effectiveness of prayer and meditation. Solutions for life's problems are by-and-large spiritual in nature, for it is thought that it is spiritual solutions which can undo the patterns of Karma and astrology, and the webs we build by negative thinking.

Spiritual Frontiers, then, emphasizes spiritual explanations and solutions for everyday problems, and nondiscursive, experiential methods of learning. Yet SFF and the other metaphysical groups consider metaphysics a scientific religious philosophy. That the Fellowship wants to be aligned with science is made explicit in its statement of *Principles, Purposes, and Program,* published in 1974: "SFF takes the *scientific* attitude that all human experiences, including extrasensory perception (telepathy, clairvoyance, precognition and related phenomena) are to be studied without prejudice for better understanding of the invisible world, and the nature of man and the universe." The Fellowship states also that it "seeks to share with *science* the implications of its own method, which is the examination of all available evidence as the basis of understanding and progress."

Certain aspects of the philosophy, social organization, and rhetoric of the metaphysical groups savor of science. Spiritual Frontiers supports a Research Committee, and its *Spiritual Frontiers Journal* is published in a scholarly format. The metaphysical participants are called *students,* and the groups are *classes.* It is not belief which is discussed in the *classes,* but *theories, concepts,* or *ideas* (the *theory* of reincarnation, for example). When the *classes* end, the *students graduate.* A leader said metaphysics was concerned not with the supernatural, which is forever scientifically inexplicable, but with the "supernormal" which is not yet fully understood by science, but is amenable to eventual scientific explanation.

Fundamental to metaphysics' definition of itself as a "scientific religious philosophy" is the very metaphysical epistemology which I have taken to be nondiscursive in nature. Within the groups themselves, the metaphysical methodology for finding truth is equated with scientific thought. It is the process of relying on personal experience as the authority for truth which metaphysicians identify with science. That is, metaphysical students withhold faith until the facts of their own personal experience are in. Withholding faith until an evidential experience manifests itself is considered akin to the scientific method. "Faith, like scientific results, is not considered a state of mind but the result of direct experience."[26] Metaphysical students are expected to "test" what they read and hear and to be "skeptical" about any concept until proved in their own experience. This process of "sorting, surveying, analyzing and abstracting" described by Jenny as "deciding what to keep and what to throw out," and by a group member as "picking and choosing for yourself" and "filing away" what is not now understood or accepted, "resembles, and not by coincidence, the intellectual democracy of the scientific or academic community."[27] The "free marketplace of ideas" is seen as similar to the intellectual freedom of science.

There are, of course, some very real differences between the way scientists and metaphysicians use "experience" to verify their propositions. First, the propositions to be verified are different in nature. One of the defining characteristics of a "spiritual" proposition, such as "God is within" is that it cannot be tested by observing with the senses, as can, for example, the second law of thermodynamics. Secondly, a scientific experiment can be replicated by other researchers. The results are objective and are publicly verifiable. The nondiscursive experiences which validate spiritual propositions are subjective, personal and often ineffable. This is not to say that they do not happen, or that they are not "real," but one person's nondiscursive "experience" is not another's.

There are other kinds of personal experiences, besides intense religious experience, which are taken to be proofs of metaphysical claims. For example, feeling better after "having a healing" is proof of the efficacy of healing. Buying things you want at bargain prices after tithing is proof of the "Law of Cause and Effect" ("you have to give to receive"). While not as "internal" as a meditative state (i.e., "healings" can be verified medically, and whether something is a bargain is a substantive question), these are no better than "correlations." The scientist would not accept them as proofs, because he could not trace the causal links.

Summary Conclusion

The alleviation of individual meaninglessness through self-realization is a primary function of the Spiritual Frontiers Fellowship and metaphysical groups like it. Spiritual Frontiers Fellowship's response to meaninglessness serves to support contemporary American cultural values, in accord with Judah's observation that the metaphysical movements are a "mirror of American culture."[28] The Fellowship expresses and legitimates individual autonomy through its philosophy of individual exegesis and the internalization of authority, while it supports a democratic decentralized structure and an anti-authoritarian leadership style. Instead of developing a countercultural community, this group celebrates the mainstream American values of individualism and democracy.

The means for establishing personal identity, or self-realization, is called "spiritual growth" and is focused on the central hypothesis that God dwells within the souls of human beings. Spiritual growth is an effective way of finding meaning because the God within, with which the aspirant identifies, is a spiritual concept, not subject to falsification. The mechanisms for spiritual growth—prayer and meditation—are nondiscursive ways of knowing. Meditation can provide the sense of union, or "just being," which obliterates distinctions between "self" and "other" and promotes an identification with all that lives. In a more down-to-earth vein, the ultimate state of "at-one-ment" is manifested in an enhanced self-image, a healthier physical state, and more positive attitudes and relationships with others.

The pragmatic aspects of the metaphysical movements support Zaretsky and Leone's conclusion that "the popular revival (of religious movements) is . . . an interest people have in improving themselves and their lives. It is a variant on how to win friends and influence people, how to bring up your child, and how to do a thousand other necessary human tasks."[29] Looked at in this light, the metaphysical movements may seem less a religion, than therapy in a spiritual idiom. They could be seen as part of the "human potential movement," which includes all sorts of "self-enhancement" groups, some of which are secular, and others spiritual, in orientation.

That Fellowship is largely a "mirror of American culture," reflecting individualism and pragmatism, makes it attractive to people who want to improve themselves—who want to fill the void left by the feeling that "there must be something more to life"—but who do not want to make major changes in their lifestyles. SFF does not reject the values the "middle American" brings into the group. It does not require that members remove themselves from the mainstream of American society. Indeed, their acquired spiritual power and enhanced sense of self are meant to help them improve their position in that society. While metaphysical students report major changes in identity and sense of well-being, life-rending changes in lifestyle and physical comforts need not be made. Vegetarianism, celibacy, refutation of material goods, are not required. Spiritually mature persons are not saints; they are a success at their job and on good terms with their neighbors. This spiritual "community" also does not burden its followers with demands for their money or their time. The only support fellow travelers on the path to spiritual growth require is spiritual support. This strong emphasis on individualism, perhaps to the detriment of "community," has caused social critics to decry a trend toward "narcissism."[30]

But Spiritual Frontiers Fellowship offers both a genuine search for meaning and practical ways of dispelling guilt or dealing with hypertension and drinking. Answers to life's grandest philosophical questions can be found in the metaphysical milieu; and these answers are presented in much more specific detail and proffered in a more optimistic tone than those espoused by the Methodist or Baptist minister

from the pulpit. Solutions for life's most mundane irritations—
headaches, backaches, little sons who won't take naps—
are also found in metaphysics. Indeed, the Study Group
offered ways of curtailing the hostility caused by the
"toothpaste tube squeezed in the middle," ways of alleviat-
ing physical pain, and things to do for things we can do
nothing about. A "pessimistic" concept of sin and an awe-
some angry God, are far from the metaphysical construction
of reality. Rather, anyone who follows a path to spiritual
growth will achieve salvation, or "at-one-ment," with the
divine inner self. There is no wrongdoing which cannot be
forgiven (by mortal and supernatural alike). Most unpleasant situations encountered by humans can be "changed"
through prayer, meditation, or positive thinking. But even if
"things" can't be changed, the burdens of anxiety and guilt
can still be lifted by "giving them to God," or by accepting
that "this is the way it's supposed to be for this life."

Metaphysics is a working-out, in the religious sphere,
of the American celebration of personal autonomy. The
Fellowship's emphasis on individualism and self-realization
is reminiscent of the "invisible" religion that Luckmann
speculates will emerge in modern society.[31] Spiritual Frontiers is an ultimately modern adaptation to society's frag-
mentation. Rather than turning back toward a small and
structured *Gemeinschaft*, the Fellowship carried a *gesell-
schaftlich* sense of freedom into the realm of religion. The
metaphysical groups recognize the new freedom and give
moderns an anchor from within. "Overchoice" is assuaged
because the metaphysicians have the means to look within
themselves and discover which of the barrage of principles
and ideas "make sense" and which will help them to inte-
grate their lives. In the context of a supportive, but non-
communal and non-enduring fellowship, individuals seek
their own path to a spiritual "truth" which enables them to
ponder the mysteries of life and death.

NOTES

1 The most valuable source of information about these groups is provided by J. Stillson Judah, *The History and Philosophy of the Metaphysical Movements in America* (Philadelphia: Westminster, 1967). See also J. Gordon Melton, *A Directory of Religious Bodies in the United States* (New York: Garland, 1977).

2 See Thomas Robbins, Dick Anthony and James Richardson, "Theory and Research in Today's New Religions," *Sociological Analysis*, 39, no. 2 (Summer 1978): 95-122; also Orrin E. Klapp, *Collective Search for Identity* (New York: Holt, Rinehart & Winston, 1969).

3 See Robert N. Bellah, *Beyond Belief* (New York: Harper & Row, 1970), and Alvin Toffler, *Future Shock* (New York: Random House, 1970).

4 See Robert Galbreath, "Introduction: The Occult Today," *Journal of Popular Culture*, 5, no. 3 (1971): 629-34; also Marcello Truzzi, "The Occult Revival as Popular Culture: Some Random Observations on the Old and Nouveau Witch," *Sociological Quarterly*, 13 (Winter 1972): 16-36.

5 Truzzi, p. 36.

6 See Clifford Geertz, "Religion as a Cultural System," in Michael Banton, ed., *Anthropological Approaches to the Study of Religion* (London: Tavistock Publications, 1966).

7 See Martin Marty, "The Occult Establishment," *Social Research*, 37, no. 2 (Summer 1970): 212-30.

8 Among the sources of information available from the National Office at Independence, Missouri, is the 1974 volume: *Spiritual Frontiers Fellowship: Its Principles, Purposes and Programs*. In 1971 the organization distributed a handbook: *A Guidebook on Policy and Practice for the Use of National Council and Committee Members and of Local Chairmen, Officers and Committees*.

9 Judah, p. 15.

10 *Ibid.*, p. 13.

11 See Harriet Whitehead, "Reasonably Fantastic: Some Perspectives on Scientology, Science Fiction, and Occultism," in Irving I. Zaretzky and Mark P. Leone, eds., *Religious Movements in Contemporary America* (Princeton: Princeton University Press, 1974), pp. 547-87.

12 Arthur Ford, "A Force or a Farce," Lecture at Annual National Conference (Evanston, Ill.: Spiritual Frontiers Fellowship, 1967).

13 Whitehead, p. 559. See also Roy Wallis, "Reflections on When Prophecy Fails," *The Zetetic: Newsletter of Academic Research into Occultisms*, 4, no. 1 (1975): 9-14.

14 Truzzi.

15 *A Guidebook on Policy and Practice*, pp. 34-35.

16 Lawrence Althouse, "The President's Corner: Swansong from a Lame Duck?" *Newsletter* of Spiritual Frontiers Fellowship, 10, no. 5 (1976). See also Patricia Hayes, *Know Yourself* (Miami: Patricia Hayes, 1971).

17 Charles Fair, *The New Nonsense: The End of the Rational Consensus* (New York: Simon and Schuster, 1974).

18 Hayes, p. 24.

19 See Jacob Needleman, *The New Religions* (New York: E.P. Dutton, 1970); also Robert S. Ellwood, Jr., *Religious and Spiritual Groups in Modern America* (Englewood Cliffs, N.J.; Prentice-Hall, 1973); and Judah.

20 See Jan van Baal, *Symbols for Communication: An Introduction to the Anthropological Study of Religion* (Assen, the Netherlands: Koninklijke Van Gorcum, 1971).

21 See James Fernandez, "The Mission of Metaphor in Expressive Culture," *Current Anthropology*, 15 (1974): 119-45.

22 Irving I. Zaretsky and Mark P. Leone, eds., "The Common Foundation of Religious Diversity," *Religious Movements in Contemporary America* (Princeton: Princeton University Press, 1974), pp. xvii-xxxvi.

23 Hayes, pp. 90-91.

24 Judah, p. 11.

25 Paul L. Higgins, "Spiritual Frontiers Fellowship: History of its First Ten Years," *Gateway*, Journal of the Spiritual Frontiers Fellowship, 11, no. 7 (1966): 161-68.

26 Zaretsky and Leone, p. xxx.

27 Whitehead, p. 560.

28 Judah, pp. 21-49, also Zaretsky and Leone, p. xxvi.

29 Zaretsky and Leone, p. xx.

30 See Joseph H. Fichter, "The Trend to Spiritual Narcissism," *Commonweal*, March 17, 1978, pp. 169-73; also Christopher Lasch, *The Culture of Narcissism* (New York: Norton, 1978); and Peter Marin, "The New Narcissism," *Harper's*, October 1975, pp. 45-56.

31 Thomas Luckmann, *The Invisible Religion: The Problem of Religion in Modern Society* (New York: Macmillan, 1967).

Thelemic Magick in America

J. Gordon Melton

Though frequently overlooked by students of the so-called "new" religions in America, the occult community seems to serve many people as an alternative to the conventional religious systems of belief and worship. Populated by Spiritualists, Theosophists, Flying Saucer devotees, psychedelic drug users, and occult fraternities and sisterhoods, it · has supplied a continuing thread of alternative spiritual perspective and practice since the early colonial period. Most of these are occult mystics, falling roughly into the category of the American metaphysical movement, ranging from conventional psychics to groups involved in witchcraft and magic.

This paper offers a brief historical account of the American development of one psychic group, the *Ordo Templi Orientis*[*]which featured the inclusion of sex magick within the wider range of occult practices.[1] It varied most, however, from traditional hermetic and alchemical magical groups by its adoption of the "thelemic magick" of Aleister Crowley. The concept of *thelema* (Greek for will) was derived from the fictional Abbey of Theleme, described in Rabelais' satirical biography of Gargantua.[2] At this Abbey the monastic vows were abolished. The only rule was "do what thou wilt" with the logical consequence that thelemite and libertine became synonymous terms. Crowley, however, interpreted this slogan to mean that every person has a true will, a destiny, a purpose, a suitable orbit for correct individual behavior. The whole intent of thelemic training is to learn how to conform to this true will. All magical practice, including sex magick, is directed to that single goal.

---

*Publisher's Note Publication of this article in no way implies that the publishers consider the Ordo Templi Orientis a legitimate alternative.

The Revival of Magick

On the outer edge of the occult community stand the practitioners of magic—Witches, Neo-Pagans and the elite corps of ritual or ceremonial magicians (not to be confused with professional tricksters like Harry Houdini). By the beginning of the nineteenth century, due largely to the technological and scientific de-sacralization of nature, magick had all but disappeared in the West.[3] During the 1970s new varieties of magicians emerged from near oblivion to become a noticeable presence in some American urban centers. In fact, the current revival of magical activity marks a dramatic reversal of a long-term trend.

At the point when it had almost disappeared in mid-nineteenth century, magick suddenly found a few followers among students of the occult. These persons, especially Francis Barrett and Eliphas Levi, recovered the magical vision of transformation.[4] After jettisoning the obsolete alchemical model and much of the old-fashioned supernaturalism, they began to construct a new magical system. Employing a "scientific" model drawn from Mesmerism, they identified magic with the use of animal magnetic forces. In the last half of the century, several secret magical groups were formed in England, and out of these groups there arose Aleister Crowley (1875-1947), the great prophet acknowledged by modern magicians as the major impetus for the contemporary magical revival.[5]

Crowley's career spans the first half of the twentieth century. Born of Plymouth Brethren parents, he rejected their fundamentalist faith as a teenager, but when he began independent magical work, he introduced a key item of fundamentalist Christianity: dispensationalism. The theory that history evolves in a series of stages, or dispensations, traces back to Joachim of Fiore, and has been picked up and revised by many others, notably Hegel and Schilling, more recently by the Unificationists. The version taught by John Nelson Darby, founder of the Plymouth Brethren, was reinterpreted by Crowley after his magical encounter with a spirit entity named Aiwass.

The message from Aiwass came through automatic writing during a series of magical rituals conducted by Crowley in Cairo in 1904, and became known as the *Liber Legis*. This book announced also the coming of the post-Christian stage of history, the New Aeon of Horus, the Son. This Aeon, or dispensation, was to replace that of Osiris, the dying and rising God, whom Crowley identified with Christ.[6] Aiwass appointed Crowley the prophet of the New Aeon, a role he did not always enjoy. Nevertheless, he promulgated the thelemic gospel proclaiming the end of the Old Aeon. He took the name of the Beast 666 from the scriptures as a sign of his rejection of Christianity.[7] Crowley led his followers in symbolic acts of transition from the Old to the New and in casting off many of the behavioral rules governing society and religion.

Crowley was first associated with the Hermetic Order of the Golden Dawn, an occult group usually credited with the launching of the new era of magical practice. He broke with this group and formed his own order, the *Argentinum Astrum*. Then in 1912 a German occultist, Theodore Ruess, introduced Crowley to the concept of magical sexual practice, a concept he enthusiastically adopted and integrated into the heart of his magical system. At this level of magick, sex is used to produce and focus the magician's power, and under Crowley's influence it soon became a major, if not the dominant, theme in the magical revival. The thelemic gospel, made functional with sexual magick, became the basis of an integrated system of beliefs as well as an organization of devotees, though Crowley would attract relatively few faithful followers up to the time of his death in 1947.

This paper will now trace the thin magical thread that began with Crowley's remote predecessors, became focused in the occult order he developed, and all but disappeared again in the years just before the Second World War. The thread loosely binds a small band of occultists working not just on the edge of the larger secular community but on the edge of the occult community itself. Thelemites were essentially strangers and outsiders to other occultists. They propagated their doctrines in the face of a hostile environment sustained by a vision of themselves as the progenitors of a new gospel for the dawning age of humanity.

The Brotherhood of Eulis

While popular myth traces the emergence of Western sex magick to the practices of the tantric yogis of India, the actual sources of these practices are much more mundane. They descended generally from American Spiritualism, but more particularly from one Pascal Beverly Randolph, a descendent of the Randolphs of Virginia, who founded the *Fraternitas Rosea Crucis* in 1858 and established the first lodge three years later. Randolph established himself as a popular occult writer in the 1860s and was a participant in the heated occultist controversies over family, marriage, sex and the role and rights of women. From the beginnings of their movement in the 1840s, Spiritualists had disseminated an "occult" perspective of sexual life and conduct. Andrew Jackson Davis, sanctioned by Spirit, had proclaimed that:

> Love is developed from the blood. . . . That ultimate essence of the blood to which reference has been made is the sacred menstrum of love, the seminal secretion, the seed of life which flows through the system.[9]

Other Spiritualists, most notably Victoria Woodhull, related the occult with issues of sexual freedom and with the attack on Victorian sexual mores. At one point in 1872 Randolph was arrested and tried for publishing explicit sexual materials, which now seem rather dull treatises about his peculiar philosophy of love and physical attraction. Within the Brotherhood of Eulis, the Rosicrucian inner court, Randolph could and did go much further. Despite denials of

those who succeeded him in the leadership of the Rosicrucian Fraternity, he taught the principles of sexual magick
and built a total occult system on a sexual model. While
drawing on Western occult materials, Randolph also claimed
Arabic origins and said that he had learned from a dusky
Arabic maiden, indirectly and by suggestion:

> the fundamental principle of the White Magick of Love; subse-
> quently, I became affiliated with some dervishes and fakirs of
> whim, by suggestion still, I found the road to other knowledges.
>
>   The Rosicrucian system is, and never was other else
> than a door to the ineffable Grand Temple of Eulis. It was the
> trial chamber wherein men were tested as to their fitness for
> loftier things.

To the members of the Fellowship of Eulis, Randolph
proclaimed that his brand of White Magick prescribed a
polarization of the human soul as a force within each human
body. The negative (masculine) aspect was centered in the
brain, and the positive (feminine) in the genital region.
Through the positive pole of our soul we can contact the
foundation fire of the Universe and the creative aspects of
life: emotion, beauty, energy and growth. Through Love one
can come into rapport with the very arterial blood of God
and, as Randolph asserted, the feminine is nearer God than
the masculine. The implications for magical sexual activity
are obvious.

After Randolph's death in 1875, his American disciples
gradually died out. His successors as head of the Rosicrucian
Fraternity did not follow his sexual teachings. He had
succeeded, however, in transmitting his ideas and practices
to a group of French students who continue his work into
modern times.[10] Twenty years later, in 1895, Karl Kellner, a
Viennese occultist, founded the *Ordo Templi Orientis*. He
claimed that the sexual magical practices derived from three
adepts, one Arab and two Hindu, but there is no evidence of
either Sufi (Arab) or tantric (Hindu) teachings in anything
Kellner passed on to his followers. It is probable that Kellner

picked up the sex magick from Randolph's French disciples
without acknowledging the connection, a practice still quite
common in occult circles to this day.

After Kellner's death in 1905, Theodore Reuss became
Outer Head of the Order and as such introduced the secret
sexual teachings to Aleister Crowley, then head of the minis-
cule *Argentinum Astrum* which he had formed after his
break with the Hermetic Order of the Golden Dawn. Reuss
appointed Crowley head of the British Order, and Crowley
set out to explore all of the possibilities of this new magical
model. He molded the Order into the main organization
teaching and promoting the practice of sex magick in the
West. Through Crowley the practice would return to the
United States where it began with Randolph.

Ordo Templi Orientis

The major stream of modern magick, as represented by
the *Ordo Templi Orientis,* came to America in the person of
Charles Stansfeld Jones, more popularly known by his magical name, Frater Achad. Achad had been introduced to
magic by J.F.C. Fuller (Frater Per Ardua) and in 1909 became a probationer in Crowley's *Argentinum Astrum.* After
Crowley formed the British branch of the Order, Achad also
joined it and quickly moved up through the lower degrees.
As World War I approached, Achad returned to his native
Canada and settled in Vancouver where in 1913 he began to
organize a magical group. Meanwhile, in 1914, Aleister
Crowley optimistically sailed for New York where he hoped
to be the ''founder of a new and greater Pagan cult.''[11]
Within weeks of Crowley's arrival, Achad sent twelve proba-
tioners to New York City to be initiated by him. Crowley,
however, diverted from full-time magick by lack of money,
had to take a job with the *International* and the *Fatherland,*
two German propaganda magazines.

In 1915 Crowley began serious magical activities and
in the fall equinox initiated his first experiments in sex

magick with Jane Foster, whose magical name was Hilarion. Their schedule of magical sex rituals was designed to produce a magical son, specifically the one who had been prophesied in the *Liber Legis*. The spirit entity, Aiwass, did not prophesy that a physical child would be born of Crowley's magical consort, Hilarion, but that if the *Liber Legis* were properly followed there would appear: "one (who) cometh after him, whence I say not, who shall discover the key of it all." Aiwass had told Crowley that this magical successor would explain all the mysteries of the Book.

Meanwhile, in Vancouver, Frater Achad had been granted an honorary X° (the administrative degree), thus commissioning him to establish the first Canadian Lodge of the Order. At the summer solstice of 1916, just nine months after Crowley's sexual magick with Hilarion in New York, Frater Achad underwent a magical initiation which included his assumption of the grade of Master of the Temple, the position then held by Crowley. During the week after the solstice, Achad continually speculated on his new status and eventually arrived at the conclusion that he was the son mentioned in *The Book of The Law*, the "one" who would come after Crowley to explain its hidden parts. He telegraphed his conclusion to Crowley.

Crowley did not at first understand Achad's claim. He was distracted by his own struggle upward from Master of the Temple to the status of Magus. To Crowley such a move would demand his total identification with the Law (i.e., the revelation given to him by Aiwass) and the total commitment of his life to its promulgation to the exclusion of all other aims. Achad had, in part, taken the oath of a Master of the Temple and asserted his new status because he believed that Crowley was looking for someone to hold that position before he could move to Magus.

The ongoing relationship between Achad and Crowley now became crucial to the future of the fledgling Order as it attempted to grow on American soil. Crowley accepted

Achad as his magical son and then proclaimed himself a Magus. In December 1917 Achad underwent a second deep magical experience in which he discovered the "key" to *Liber Legis*. He then moved to New York to join Crowley who gave him a new name, "Arctaeon," as an acknowledged Exempt Adept. Crowley also gave an inscribed copy of a new book, *Liber Aleph*, to his new magical son and offered it as an extensive guide to the traveler on the magical path. After several months, Achad suggested that he had possibly jumped a grade and, surpassing Crowley, could now be considered an *Ipsissimus*—the single grade higher than Magus. Crowley, of course, rejected the suggestion out of hand and relations between them were never the same again.[12]

As relations between the two magicians cooled, Achad moved to Chicago where he gave weekly lectures for several years and published several of his most important books.[13] Crowley, as Achad's thinking deviated more from his own, disowned him as a magical offspring. He questioned Achad's unbroken succession to the grade of Master of the Temple. He relegated Achad to the depths commenting, "thus Parzival (Achad) is a Fool, to look at from below, and I am a Magus."[14] Crowley, apart from Achad, continued to practice and explore the sexual magick begun with Hilarion. He changed female partners frequently, often buying the services of prostitutes for an evening of magical rituals. Towards the end of his American stay, he met and took as his Scarlet Woman, Leah Hirsig, who went with him to Sicily, where he established his "Abbey of Thelema" at Cefalu. Some of his American disciples—people such as Israel Regardie, Jane Wolfe and Dorothy Olson—travelled to Europe to spend time with Crowley or corresponded with him and took instruction individually by mail.

In the mid-1920s Karl Germer, a German disciple, arrived in New York City for an extended visit with the main objective to raise money and oversee the publication of

Crowley's books. In November 1928 he met Cora Eaton, a possible source of a subsidy loan, whom he married early the next year after divorcing his first wife. They returned to Europe after arranging for the publication and distribution of *Magic in Theory and Practice,* one of Crowley's most important books.

Meanwhile, Dorothy Olson, who had briefly been Crowley's Scarlet Woman, one of his sex magick partners, returned to the United States and settled in Chicago. She kept up a steady correspondence with Crowley but could report no success in building up the Order. Achad's years in Chicago had stimulated the occult community, but Dorothy could not even get the local occult bookstore to carry Crowley's books. Like Dorothy, Jane Wolfe, a disciple in Hollywood, reported financial difficulties which hampered her activities. She worked with others in trying to establish an Order group, but had to report to Germer in early 1930:

> The situation here looks rather good for the Law (i.e., Crowley's teachings), but not for organization as yet. A strong, big personality is needed for anything of a public character for large numbers. Smith dreams and dreams and yearns over the O.T.O. There is opportunity for out-door ritual but at present only a saccharine rigamarole would be acceptable— Pilgrimage Plays and the like. The climate is ideal for rites. This is my dream also. Rites out in the hills.[15]

The dreams would soon materialize. In 1934 Smith incorporated a Church of Thelema with himself as Rex Summus Sanctissimus and *The Book of The Law* as the doctrinal authority. By 1936 Smith began gathering a group that later became known as the Agape Lodge of the Order. At this time Crowley was having his own troubles. Mussolini had expelled him from Italy; financial problems plagued him in England; the Nazis were suppressing the occult in Germany; and Smith's tiny Agape Lodge in Los Angeles soon became the only organized thelemic group in the world.

The Agape Lodge

Smith and another Frater who was his co-worker at the Southern California Gas Company built up the Agape Lodge to include an active membership of over eighty devotees. Each Sunday evening they conducted a performance of a Gnostic Mass, the text of which Crowley wrote and to which the public was invited. News reporters described these events and interviewed local residents from whom they learned of an alleged "immoral relationship" involving three members living at the Lodge. The subsequent published article brought unwanted notoriety. Smith and his partner were demoted from their jobs, and most of the membership resigned from the Lodge.

The reduced membership of the Agape Lodge continued its quiet existence and did not begin to grow again in numbers until the advent of Jack Parsons in 1939. He was a research chemist, a man of great energy and imagination and one of the founders of the Jet Propulsion Laboratory at the California Institute of Technology. He proposed that they rent a large residence and create their own Abbey of Thelema, thus allowing Smith to assume full-time leadership of the group.

In the highly charged emotional atmosphere of the Abbey, which included both the additional pressures on the members involved in magical training and the ego development implicit in the thelemic philosophy, relationships began to fracture. In thelemic groups, one tends to do sex magick with a single magical partner, usually one's spouse. After the Abbey was established, however, the rituals of sexual magick began to involve multiple partners. Regina Kahl, Smith's partner, moved to Texas, and he began to do his rituals with Parsons' wife by whom he fathered a child. Parsons, in turn, took Betty, his former wife's sister, in magical partnership.

Parsons soon complained to Crowley that Smith was becoming lax in his duties at the Abbey. Crowley reacted and chose to handle the problem with a uniquely magical method. He wrote *Liber 132* in which he related that Smith, because of his unusual astrological chart, was not a human being at all, but the incarnation of some god. Therefore, said Crowley, Smith should begin an immediate magical retirement during which he was to discover the identity of the god dwelling within him. Smith obediently moved to a quiet country place where he experienced the ''Mark of the Beast'' on his body. He had little contact with other members of the Order, but reported to Karl Germer, who had moved to New York after his escape from the Nazis.

Meanwhile, Jack Parsons became acting head of the Agape Lodge in Pasadena and continued to work sexual magick with his new consort, Betty, but was unwilling, or unable, to bring more converts into the movement. In 1945, at the end of the Second World War, Parsons formed a friendship with L. Ron Hubbard,* an ex-naval officer, writer of pulp fiction, undercover agent, amateur philosopher and theologian, and later founder of the Church of Scientology.[16] Hubbard began to frequent the Lodge and Betty attached herself to him. His friendship with Parsons did not seem disrupted by this switch of allegiance on Betty's part. Hubbard never joined the Lodge, but he assisted Parsons in a series of magical rituals, with the intention of locating a new magical partner for Parsons. During one of these they encountered a spirit entity they identified as Wilfred Smith. Parsons used his expertise to pin Smith's body to the temple door with four throwing knives. Soon after these rituals Marjorie Cameron appeared. She became Parsons' new magical sex partner and eventually his wife. He and Hubbard took her arrival as confirmation of their course of action.

---

*Publisher's Note The Church of Scientology maintains that L. Ron Hubbard was not spiritually connected to the OTO. His only connection to the OTO was through his investigation of it as a part of his job as a member of the Los Angeles Police Department which requested the investigation. As a police officer, Mr. Hubbard assisted one woman who wanted to leave the group.

Once Candy (as Marjorie became known) settled in, Parsons began a set of sexual magick rituals with the intention of producing the magical child that Achad had failed to be. Seeing Candy as the Scarlet Woman, Parsons hoped to produce the one who would unlock the hidden messages of *The Book of The Law*. During the course of these rituals, Hubbard acted as a clairvoyant describing the happenings on the astral. Parsons was convinced that he had now contacted the spirit entity, Babalon, who was mentioned in *The Book of The Law* and that from this contact the magical child destined to lead all humanity to true freedom would appear nine months later.

The events of the next nine months produced quite the opposite results for Parsons. He and Hubbard, after a series of both personal and business disagreements, had a complete break in their relationship. Crowley, learning through his voluminous correspondence with California thelemites of Parsons' activities, felt that he was pursuing dangerous paths. He appointed Grady McMurtry (Frater Hymanaeus Alpha), a member of the Lodge he had met during World War II, as his representative to investigate and reform the situation if necessary. Along with Germer, McMurtry conducted an investigation which produced no conclusions, only a heightened distrust among those involved. The break with Hubbard, the rebuke from Crowley, and the actions of McMurtry and Germer greatly weakened Parsons' position in the movement. At this point the owner of the Pasadena building, rented by the Lodge, ordered their eviction so that he could demolish the building and replace it with a hotel. With this action, the California Abbey of Theleme ceased to exist. Headquarters of the Lodge moved to Parsons' residence, but the interest waned and the Lodge never recovered.

The Germer Era

After the death of Crowley in 1947, when Germer became the acknowledged head of the *Ordo Templi Orientis,*

Parsons continued as leader of the Agape Lodge and revived the working of magick which he had ceased after the
break with Hubbard. For circulating thelemic materials on
the campus of the California Institute of Technology, he was
suspended for a period from his position there in 1948. In
the course of further magical ritual, he again encountered
the astral entity Babalon, who posed for him the choice of
crossing the Abyss, the magical experience that leads to the
higher grades of magical attainment. The Abyss forces the
magician to encounter his/her deepest darkest side, but only
by this experience can one attain the grade of Master
magician.

Parsons reported that after forty days "in the madness
and horror of the Abyss," he took the oath of Antichrist in
the presence of Frater 132 (Wilfred Smith) with whom he
again had resumed contact. In taking this oath as the embodi-
ment of "Antichrist," Parsons was assuming Crowley's position as the prophet of the New Aeon. As the agent of
transition he not only destroys the Old Aeon, personified in
the "pretense and lying hypocrisy of Christianity" and its
"servile virtues and superstitious restrictions," but brings
the message of the New Aeon. This later task he accomplished by producing an additional chapter for *The Book of
The Law,* called *The Book of Babalon.* He predicted that the
nation would accept this law within nine years, but he did
not live long enough to experience the failure of his prophecy. His program failed to gain the support of his fellow
magicians. The end came suddenly in 1952 when Parsons
was killed while experimenting with explosives in the make-
shift laboratory of his Pasadena home.

Meanwhile, the mantle of leadership had been picked
up by Crowley's immigrant friend and financial supporter,
Karl Germer, termed by historian Francis King as "the most
interesting and certainly the most important member of the
German Section of the *Ordo Templi Orientis.*"[17] An early
interest in magick was intensified in the early 1920s when

Crowley came to Europe to develop the international out-
reach of the Order. Germer then working for a Munich
publisher helped to translate and publish several of Crowley's
short items in German. His involvement with the Crowley
magicians grew to the point that, with the help of his second
wife, he established the Thelema Verlag, a publishing company in Leipzig.

The emergence of rightist dictatorships that had made
Crowley's magical activities unpopular in Europe, also had
an effect on Germer's efforts, both in publication and
organization. He was arrested by the Gestapo in 1935 and
imprisoned for seven months in Esterwegen Concentration
Camp, where he had a vision of his Holy Guardian Angel.
After his release he settled in Belgium attempting to hold
the scattered thelemic flock together. In 1941 when Belgium was occupied by the Nazis, the authorities arrested
him and deported him to France, from which he finally
made his way back to the United States.

Crowley had earlier appointed Germer "Grand Trea-
surer" of the *Ordo Temple Orientis* because of his proclivity
for raising money, a task which he performed with greater
efficiency than he demonstrated in the organizational activities among the membership. Shortly after Crowley's death
in 1947, Germer proclaimed himself Outer Head of the
Order, an action that irritated the ninth degree American
members who had assumed that they would hold an election to name the new leader and successor to Crowley. At his
headquarters in New York, Germer was isolated from the
American members in California, as well as from the European members who were relatively disorganized after the
World War. During the fifteen years of his leadership he
refused to initiate any new members into the Order, nor had
he named, or arranged for, a successor at the time of his
death in 1962.

The end of the "Germer Era" was also the end of the
semblance of unity that Crowley had established within his

loosely organized fellowship of thelemic magicians. After Parsons' death only two small groups remained, one in London led by Kenneth Grant, who had refused to stop work when Germer revoked his charter, and one in Switzerland led by Karl Metzger. In 1965 the future of the Order appeared extremely bleak, but some individual thelemites were reading Crowley's books that were circulating through the occult community, and before the decade was out at least four groups emerged to continue the work.

In the mid-1960s Georgina and Richard Brayton, former members of the Agape Lodge, established the Solar Lodge in Los Angeles and operated the Eye of Horus Book Store near the campus of the University of Southern California. This venture was, however, short-lived as the Lodge disintegrated in a police raid and the arrest and conviction of eleven members on various charges (none of which had to do with the working of magick).[18] Secondly, Grady McMurtry, the main claimant to the Crowley legacy, began in 1969 to reconstruct an American Order. From a small handful of people, this branch now includes lodges across the United States.

Thirdly, Macelo Motta, a Brazilian member of the *OTO* asserted his right to leadership on the simple grounds that "there is no one else to do it." He established an American section in Nashville in 1979 and developed a vigorous publishing effort, Troll Press. He not only published much Crowley material, but has revived *The Equinox*, Crowley's old magazine, each issue of which is the size of a large book. During its first two years Motta instituted a number of lodges in American cities. Finally, even after Germer revoked the charter of Kenneth Grant's lodge in London, Grant continued to build his movement. In the 1970s he established himself and his groups firmly in America and is now in competition with McMurtry.

The revival of interest in thelemic magick includes far more than the continuing remnants of the *Ordo Templi*

Orientis. During the 1970s two old occult publishing houses, Samuel Weiser and Llywellyn, began to put Crowley into print again and found a ready market. Several new publishing houses (Level Press, 93 Publishing, Sangreal, and Unicorn) were established primarily to publish thelemic material. Independent thelemites such as Gerald Kelly, publisher of *The Newaeon,* began issuing thelemic periodicals. Other thelemic groups such as the Chicago based Monastery of the Seven Rays, the Ordo Adeptorum Invisiblum (London and Chicago), the Ordo Templi Dianos (Ohio), the Ordo Templi Wand (Connecticut), and the Order of Thelema (San Diego) now spread their version of Crowley's gospel.

Thus the thin thread of activity that began with Randolph, continued with Crowley, Parsons and Germer and all but died in 1962 is emerging in the 1980s as a small but growing alternative within the occult community. There appears to be little possibility, however, that this type of erotic magick can become a popular alternative to America's organized religions.

Summary Conclusion

The relationship between religion and magick has long intrigued the modern student of religion especially in the technological, rational and scientistic countries of the West where secularists tend to be suspicious that both magick and religion are rife with superstition. Malinowski's classic work among the primitives has provided clear distinctions and definitions known to every college student.[19] Yinger points out that:

> to the scientific observer, the magical way of thinking is invalid and ineffective. Based as it is on crude analogies and false inference, magic certainly does not "work." Why then is it not quickly dismissed because of its failure? The answer to that is twofold: to the believer it *seems* to work; and to some degree, in an indirect sense, it does work. This ques-

tion is interesting to the student of religion, not only because of the frequency with which magical elements are found in religious systems, but also because some of the same reasoning applies to religion.[20]

The magick of Thelema is truly an alternative to religion; its relations and functions are substitutes for those which religion provided. Magick is essentially superstitious because it attributes "powers" to an object or person which cannot be so attributed. In the Christian tradition of Western culture the thelemic sexual rituals between two unmarried persons are obviously adulterous, and the use of sex magick to produce and focus the magician's power is obviously imaginary. These rituals which are intended to direct the human will (the thelematic faculty) toward its true destiny, promise the rejuvenation and regeneration of the individual. Transmutation is said to allow the magician to shift the object of his, or her, sexual passion to some intangible and desirable ideal.

Although occultism is as old as history, and large varieties of occult people, practices and groups have existed in the United States, the thelemic magick discussed in this chapter was brought from Britain by Aleister Crowley. The story of its development is his story. The sacred scripture of the movement, the *Liber Legis,* was dictated to Crowley by the spirit entity, Aiwass, although the doctrines contained therein carry traces of Rosicrucian thought, evolved through the Brotherhood of Eulis, and became specific to Crowley when the secret sexual practices of the *Ordo Templi Orientis* were introduced to him by the Outer Head of the Order, Theodore Reuss.

The esoteric content of the *Liber Legis,* comprehended only by the fully initiate of the Order, included the promise of a prophetic figure who would unfold all the mysteries of the universe and thus direct the thelemites to true freedom. Two efforts are recorded of the attempt to produce this powerful entity, in one instance by Crowley and Hilarion, and another by Parsons and Marjorie. In spite of carefully performed magical sex rituals, the expected "magical child" did not appear in either case. There is here a remote analogy to the "coming of a Messiah," but the prophet in this instance is not for the redemption from sin but for the fulfillment of the willful desires of the magicians.

The practices of thelemicists can be viewed, like the practices of various yogas, as exercises in training the mind and body and grasping after spiritual reality. The spiritual quest inherent in thelemic magick is frequenly hard to grasp because of our general ignorance of its similarities with various Asian and Middle Eastern spiritual paths, in particular, Indian tantra, and because of the separation of sex and spirituality so prevalent in Western religion.[21] When westerners encounter forms of spirituality in which sex is used as a means to enhance the spiritual quest, they tend to view the practices in moral rather than religious categories.

Thus the thelemic magicians can best be seen as participants in the occult and metaphysical search for spiritual reality and of perpetuating a thread of spiritual practice going back to B.P. Randolph. Central to the account is the story of Aleister Crowley, for the development of thelemic magick really begins as he brought together traditional magic, teachings of *The Book of The Law*, the sex magick inherited from Randolph through the *OTO*, and the *OTO* organization itself. Under Crowley these became welded into a new religion with a prophet, holy book, particular form of piety and a program to change the world.

The *Ordo Templi Orientis* has a complex hierarchical system with members initiated into successive degrees of affiliation. Males are called *fraters* and females *sorores*, and they progress through a series of degrees and have access to teaching materials only up to the degree to which they are admitted. The first seven degrees teach basic magick. The eighth, ninth and eleventh involve the practice of various sex magick techniques. Those who have been admitted to the ninth degree form a ruling elite among whose powers are the choosing of a new head of the order in the case of that post's becoming vacant. The tenth degree is strictly an administrative degree for various Order functionaries.

While the degree system related to specific work accomplished and the granting of access to ever higher levels of secret teaching material, there is a separate hierarchical system related to one's level of magical occult attainment. While one can be graded and passed upon lessons and exercises which make up degree work, the accomplishments of occult attainment can only be judged by the self as they involve the acceptance of certain tasks, passing through different experiences, and the development of various elements of the self. Especially in the higher grades, the arrival at a new grade is proclaimed not granted, although usually, after a new level is reached, a magician will look to others for confirmation. In Achad's case, he looked to Crowley for confirmation that he had arrived as Master of the Temple, a fact that Crowley at first affirmed and then denied.

Today as different thelemic groups emerge, a variety of degree and grading systems have been developed. Some groups have moved away from degrees altogether since most of the secret material, especially that concerning sex magick, has been published and is available to the general public. They are also responding to the feminists issues and admitting women to all grades. Under Crowley, women could be admitted to the ninth degree, but were never recognized as having attained the higher magical grade of Master of the Temple, Magus or Ipssissimus.

Beyond participating in general in the freedoms created by the post-World War II urban environment that has promoted the spread of hundreds of alternative religions, the Order has finally found some degree of success because of two factors in particular. First, the modern climate of sexual freedom and cultural consensus that sex is primarily for pleasure have produced an environment more compatible with thelemic belief and practice. Modern thelemites are not in a constant battle with Victorian sexual repression. Secondly, the use of sophisticated birth control devices frees magicians from the distractions and fears of producing unwelcome children. Since the performance of magick requires a total concentration on the ritual intention of the magical act, it is obvious that clumsy contraceptive devices, or the worry about pregnancy, could prevent successful magical performance. These facts should allow thelemicists for the first time to test their theories and to see if they actually have, as they believe, the revealed message for our times, or whether they will remain a small group on the edge of culture.

NOTES

1 This paper is based largely on my article, "Ritual Magick," in J. Gordon Melton, *The Encyclopedia of American Religions* (Wilmington: McGrath, 1978), II: 253-63.

2 Francis Rabelais, *Gargantua*, Book I, chapters lii-lvii (New York: AMS Press, 1967), pp. 169-87.

3 See the interpretation by Robert S. Ellwood, Jr. *Religious and Spiritual Groups in Modern America* (Englewood Cliffs, N.J.: Prentice-Hall, 1973), pp. 62-128, 204-10.

4 See Christopher McIntosh, *Eliphas Levi and the French Occult Revival* (New York: Samuel Weiser, 1974); and Ellic Howe, *The Magicians of the Golden Dawn* (London: RKP, 1972).

5 On Crowley see *Francis King, The Magical World of Aleister Crowley* (New York: Coward, McCann and Geohegan, 1977).

6 For Crowley's treatment of Christ and Christianity see *Crowley on Christ*, ed. Francis King (London: Daniel, 1974).

7 Beast 666, in Revelation 13:18, has been interpreted as a future reincarnation of the Emperor Nero, first persecutor of Christians.

8 See *The Rose Cross Order* (Allentown: Philosophical Publishing, 1916); and P.B. Randolph, *Eulis, The History of Love* (McKulemne Hill: Health Research, 1961).

9 Andrew Jackson Davis, *The Harmonial Philosophy* (Milwaukee: National Spiritualist Association of Churches, n.d.), pp. 280-81.

10 See Francis King, *Sexuality, Magic and Perversion* (Secaucas, N.J.:Citadel, 1972).

11 Aleister Crowley, *Confessions* (New York: Hill and Wang, 1969), p. 792.

12 Materials on the relationship between Crowley and Achad (Jones) can be found in the mass of unpublished documents in the Crowley Collection at the Warburg Institute in London. See also "Liber CLXVI: The Master of the Temple," *Equinox*, III (March 1919): 129-70.

13 His books include: *The Egyptian Revival* (Chicago: Collegium ad Spiritum Sanctum, 1923); *Chalice of Ecstasy* (Chicago: Yogi Publication Society, 1923); *The Anatomy of the Body of God* (Chicago: Collegium ad Spiritum Sanctum, 1925).

14 See *The Magical Record of the Beast 666* (Montreal: Next Step Publications, 1972).

15 Letter from Jane Wolfe, to Karl Germer, 21 February 1930.

16 The story of Hubbard's relationship with Parsons has been a matter of great controversy, yellow journalism and numerous lawsuits. See the cautious statements of Roy Wallis, *The Road to Total Freedom* (New York: Columbia University Press, 1977), pp. 22, 111.

17 See King, *Sexuality, Magic and Perversion*, p. 119.

18 For the Solar Lodge episode see Ed Sanders, *The Family* (New York: Avon, 1972).

19 Bronislaw Malinowski, "Magic, Science and Religion," pp. 18-94, in Joseph Needham, ed., *Science, Religion and Reality* (New York: Macmillan, 1925).

20 J. Milton Yinger, *The Scientific Study of Religion* (New York: Macmillan, 1970), p. 74.

21 Cf. John Moore, *Sexuality and Spirituality* (New York: Harper & Row, 1980).

Scientology as Technological Buddhism

Frank K. Flinn

In several ways Scientology is the most interesting of the new religious movements. It describes itself as "an applied religious philosophy,"[1] but it does not fall easily under any exclusive label such as "religion," "science," "philosophy," or "technique." In a situation like this the chances are many for misclassification and misinterpretation. For the time being, some designation like "new religious movement," or "alternative religious movement," seems the most appropriate for describing these recently recognized religious phenomena.

Interpreting a New Religion

The traditional sociological classification derived from Ernst Troeltsch's *The Social Teaching of the Christian Churches* (church, denomination, sect, and cult) has encountered difficulties.[2] This is particularly true for the terms, "sect" and "cult" which have been most often applied to the newer religious groups. It is important to note that these are *relational* terms. Thus, the concept of sect takes on sharper definitional focus when related to organized churches which have become diffuse in doctrine and practice. Rodney Stark has captured this relational aspect well when he wrote that sects "reflect the efforts of the churched to remain churched."[3] The condition, then, for sect formation seems to be the presence of strongly organized churches. Conversely, the concept of cult takes on sharper definitional focus when related not to church, denomination, or sect, but to a prior condition of secularity. In Stark's words, the cult represents "efforts by the unchurched to become churched."

This definitional clarification, however, does not allow an unambiguous application of either cult or sect to Scientology. Sectarian movements are characterized by their "over againstness" to organized religion, that is, they are separated from and contrasted to other religions. Yet, one characteristic peculiar to many of the new religions—including Scientology, Unificationists, and Charismatics—is the fact that they are *pluri-denominational,* or *trans-denominational* in the religious affiliation of their adherents. Scientologists can remain in good standing as Scientologists even if they continue to participate in their natal or previously acquired religion. This is a widespread phenomenon.

A year ago I attended a gathering of the Full Gospel Businessmen's Association in St. Louis. This Pentecostal movement was started in 1952 by Demos Shakarian.[4] At one point in the meeting the people in the audience were asked to identify their religious affiliation. About one-third identified themselves as belonging to some traditional Pentecostal group. The rest were fairly evenly distributed among Episcopalians, Lutherans, Roman Catholics, Reformed Church and other mainline denominations. Conversations with these and other Pentecostals led me to think that they are not the churched striving to remain churched, but,they are the churched trying to get a spiritual dimension into their lives.

Charismatic Catholics in particular react to the traditional "propositional" faith of the catechism. They want to "feel" or "experience" their faith. Hence, their emphasis is mainly on the energizing experience of "the gifts of the Holy Spirit." Yet these Charismatic Catholics still attend traditional religious services, often with renewed fervor. Scientologists have told me similar stories about returning to their natal religious group with a new understanding of what that traditional faith was all about. Instead of "over againstness," there seems to be a "two-way traffic" between the traditional and the new in many of these movements. Post-modern faith seems to be getting *polyspheric* rather than simply "ecumenical" or, in sectarian terms, "exclusivistic." If this is sectarianism, then it is a new kind of sectarianism.

The term cult presents its own problems. If understood as the effort of the unchurched to become churched, then it may be cautiously applied to Scientology. I have conducted numerous "spiritual autobiography" interviews with Scientologists and have been astounded by the number of different religious groups they have previously joined or associated with. Most members can be described as "seekers," but their search does not have a fixed pattern. Some tried various traditional religions, others tried born-again groups, and still others had been through more esoteric astrological and meditationist affiliations. Although Scientology may be just another stage in their search, most members, when asked what Scientology did for them that their prior groups did not do, replied with the words "the tech" (auditing technology). The "tech" is "standard," i.e., authoritatively set down by L. Ron Hubbard. As we shall see further, the development of a "standard" in the technology is functionally equivalent to "infallibility" in Roman Catholicism or to the "inerrance" of Scripture in fundamentalist Protestantism. This characteristic does not correspond to "epistemological individualism" which is said to be the mark of a cult.[5] If one way of distinguishing a cult from a sect is to say that a cult is an aggregation of the "like-minded" while the sect is a congregation of the "like-committed," then Scientology falls in the camp of the sectarians.

Much of this depends upon where we are going to slice the pie. Although I do not want to say that the pie cannot or ought not to be sliced, the arbitrariness of the initial cut leaves me uneasy. I am uneasy, too, about what has happened to the word *cult* in the popular media. The popular image of a cult—a deranged, tyrannical leader, "brainwashing," bizarre beliefs and practices—may have rendered the word permanently damaged for analytic purposes. Furthermore, the word *cult* now impinges upon the legal interpretation and definition of what constitutes a religion. The U.S. constitution uses only one word—*religion*—to designate the phenomenon we are talking about. Many anti-cultists believe that they have *ipso facto* established a religious group as a "pseudo-religion" if they have managed to get the group labelled as a "cult" in court proceedings. Elsewhere I have argued that, from a constitutional viewpoint, the judiciary can only determine *that* a group is, or is not, a religion; it cannot describe *how* a group is a religion.[6] In other words, whether a group is a church, denomination, sect or cult is constitutionally irrelevant. To make distinctions like these in court proceedings would be to establish certain religions (the traditional ones) over others (the innovative ones). If making such distinctions is not an actual establishment, it certainly is *respecting* an establishment.

The above reasons convince me that we need to temper our sociological analyses with a more phenomenological and hermeneutical approach to the new religions. I take it as a primary hermeneutical principle that the interpreter must first interpret a text or tradition as it interprets itself. That is to say, I cannot presume that I understand the interpretant better than it understands itself.[7] For example, this principle states that I cannot read a religious text unless I let it in some way read me. For authentic interpretation to take place there needs to be what Hans-Georg Gadamer calls a "merging of the horizons," my own and the text's.[8] But this cannot take place unless I enter into the horizon of what the text intends and let its world of representation, categories, and figures of speech, appear and speak to my own world of representation. This reciprocal principle of interpretation does not require that I believe *what* the believer believes but asks that I take a step in the direction of believing *as* the believer believes. In the attempt to understand Islam, for example, I do not become a Muslim. But I can approximate that which is "alien" to me in the Muslim's world of representation. W. Brede Kristensen writes: "By means of empathy (the historian or interpreter) tries to relive in his own experience that which is 'alien,' and that, too, he can only approximate."[9]

The Ambiguity of Being "Clear"

Scientology bears many close resemblances to Buddhism. This affinity is part of Scientology's own self-understanding: "A Scientologist is a first cousin to the Buddhist."[10] The central Scientological term "clear" is roughly equivalent to the Buddhist concept of *bodhi* which describes "the one awake" or "enlightened one" who has gained releasement (*moksa*) from the entangling threads of existence and illusion.[11] By undergoing the auditing techniques, Scientologists hope to rid themselves of "engrams"—mental images or "facsimiles" of past pain, injury or harm which prevent the believer from being "at cause" over matter, energy, space and time (MEST).[12] In interviews, Scientologists describe the state of being "clear" as being active rather than passive over one's life situation. They also identify it with "freedom" and "awareness." Although Scientologists ascribe the discovery of the "auditing technology" to L. Ron Hubbard's independent "research," they nonetheless recognize the Buddhist tradition as part of the church's "antecedents and background." Indeed, the many levels and grades of the auditing process can be seen as a refinement and resignification of the Buddhist Eightfold Path in a space-age context.[13] In this respect, Scientology is Buddhism made applicable.

The term "clear," however, has another meaning in Scientology. It also refers to the button on the calculator which "clears" the machine of all previous entries and mistakes and allows for reprocessing of information. "Really, that is all a Clear is. Clears are beings who have been cleared of wrong answers or useless answers which keep them from living or thinking."[14] This technological image suggests that the "atomic elements" of Buddhism, obviously present in Scientology, have been transmuted into a new "molecular compound" that is characteristic of North American technologism. In *Scientology: A World Religion Emerges in the Space Age* the Buddhistic elements which coincide with Scientology are enumerated: (1) knowing for oneself, or personal experience, as the test of truth, (2) a scientific understanding of cause and effect in matters of the Spirit (*karma*), (3) Buddhism's "pragmatic" concern with human problem-solving rather than metaphysics, (4) the Middle Path which centers on Man and "the dynamics of Human development," (5) the democratic spirit in Buddhism, and (6) the emphasis on individual action.[15] Any one of these items could have been taken directly from Bacon's *Novum Organon* or William James's *Pragmatism*. Notably absent from the list, as well as from technological pragmatism, is any emphasis on meditation and contemplation.

This analysis presents a special problem. How can the realm of "religion" include what we have come to know as "technology"? The popular mind places these two concepts miles apart, but their conjunction may be a characteristic peculiar to late modernity. By "technology" I mean the linguistic union of *technē* (craft, art, making) with *logos* (word, reason, rationale) so that "knowing" is co-penetrated with "making" or "doing."[16] It is important to realize that, though the term "technology" is derived from Greek, the ancient Greek thinkers would have never joined these two words in this way. Knowing for the sake of knowing was an end in itself for the Greeks and could never be placed on the same level with "doing" or "action." "Technology" is a neologism which first came into use around 1615. Surprisingly, we discover that the Latin *technologia* made its first appearance in Puritan *theological* circles. The Puritan divine rejected the old-world *metaphysica*, by which the liberal arts were aimed in the direction of contemplation, prayer and meditation, in favor of *technologia* or the rationale of the arts aimed in the direction of *eupraxia*, right use or employment. In the New England mind, Perry Miller wrote, "technologia and theology coincided."[17]

The New England primal opening to technologia paved the royal road for the reception of Francis Bacon's new "active science" by which nature was put "under constraint and vexed...when by art and the hand of man she is forced out of her natural state and squeezed and molded."[18] Technological Baconianism is much more than "applied science" or a methodology for making useful products. It is also a mode for apprehending the world which has imbued the fundamental thrust of all North American life, including its religion. What differentiates religious fundamentalism, for example, from theological liberalism in North America is not that the former rejects the findings of science and the latter accepts them, but that the fundamentalists accepted the Baconian wave of science while the liberals accepted both Baconian empiricism *and* Darwinian evolutionism.[19] Bacon interpreted the Book of Nature as an array of "instances" whereby mankind could wrest power from natural forces, while the fundamentalists scrutinized the Book of Scripture for "evidences" whereby one could find the right formula for the conduct of life. From this perspective, Scientology may be a variation of a hybrid seed planted long ago at Plymouth Rock.

Max Weber once contrasted Buddhism and Calvinism as "ideal types" respectively of a "world-negating" and a "world-affirming" religion.[20] I think Weber's typology needs to be modified in light of a phenomenon like Scientology. Scientology has recast certain elements of Buddhism in a mold that nonetheless receives its shape from the egalitarian technologism pervasive in North American culture. Like pragmatism, the only indigenous philosophy to arise in North America, Scientology underlines the word "applied" in its self-definition as an "*applied* religious philosophy."

From Dianetics to Scientology

Before discussing the characteristics of Scientology as technological Buddhism, I need to say something about the transition from Dianetics to Scientology proper. In this regard, two of L. Ron Hubbard's writings are of paramount importance: *Dianetics: The Modern Science of Mental Health,* first published in 1950, and *Scientology: The Fundamentals of Thought,* first published in 1956. There were preliminary drafts of both works as well as intermediate writings such as *Science of Survival* (1951), but the above two books clearly mark a watershed between the two phases of the movement.

Although Dianetics has many trans-empirical and religious overtones, it falls in the category of a "mind-cure" therapy. Many commentators claim that Scientology is mental therapy masquerading as a religion. The crux of the question, however, is whether one can separate "therapy" from "religion"or even from "philosophy" by a hard-and-fast rule. The word *therapeuo* ("to heal, cure, restore") occurs frequently in the New Testament and refers to both spiritual and physical healings by Jesus of Nazareth.[21] Indeed, there seem to be many kinds of therapy, like the Platonic philosophical sequence: ignorance-conversion to dialectic-illumination, and the Christian religious sequence: sin-repentance through grace-salvation.[22] There are also many kinds of medical and psychoanalytic therapies, like the Freudian sequence: neurosis-analysis-normality; and the radical behaviorist therapy: nervous disorder-modification through psycho-tropic drugs/psychosurgery-altered behavior.

Dianetics too has its therapeutic sequence: aberration (reactive mind)-removal of engrams through auditing-"clear" (analytical mind). We shall discuss later how this sequence was modified in the Scientology phase of the movement. In terms of the therapeutic models here exemplified, Dianetics stands closer to the philosophical and religious models than to the psychoanalytic and behaviorist models. The Scientology movement in both its phases has stressed that the term "psychiatry" literally means "healing the soul" and has always opposed physicalist solutions to what members consider mental and/or spiritual problems.[23]

While Dianetics had religious and spiritual tendencies, it was not yet a religion in the full sense of the term. A number of factors can be pointed out here. First, Dianetics did not promise what may be called "transcendental" rewards as the outcome of its therapy. It did however promise "transnormal" rewards. In the book *Dianetics*, "clears" are opposed to "preclears," neophytes striving to get clear, and "normals," the person on the street. Clears do not catch colds (p. 107), and are unrepressed (p. 38), do paranormal mental computations and have "complete recall" (p. 179), have keener perceptions and improve their eyesight (p. 32), and are entirely free of "all psychoses, compulsions and repressions (all aberrations) and...any autogenic (self-generated) diseases referred to as psycho-somatic ills" (p. 30). In sum, "the dianetic clear is to a current normal individual as the current normal person is to the severely insane" (p. 15). Secondly, in the Dianetics stage of the movement, engrams were traced back to the foetal stage at the earliest (pp. 265 ff.). Thirdly, Dianetics had only four "dynamics" or "urges for survival"—self, sex, group and Mankind (p. 10). Fourthly, the auditing techniques in the Dianetics phase were fairly developed, but the "E-meter" (an electrogalvanometer commonly known as the "lie-detector" and used to gauge electrical resistance on the skin) had not come into use.

There has been much debate as to when Scientology began to be a religion. One can point to the incorporation of the Hubbard Association of Scientologists in Phoenix, Arizona, in 1952, and then to the establishment of the Founding Church of Scientology in 1954. Legal incorporation, however, does not tell us when the specifically religious concepts took shape in the church's self-understanding. These debates, however, remind one of the nineteenth century disputes on when Christianity began: during Jesus' life time? at Pentecost? through the ministry of Paul and the Apostles? I think it is more helpful to see the transition from Dianetics to Scientology in terms of the four factors discussed above.

First, the transition between the two phases of the

movement can be seen in the shift from the "trans-normal" to the "trans-empirical" or "transcendental" in the understanding of "clear." In the book *Dianetics,* a clear is defined as "the optimum individual: no longer possessed of any engrams" (p. 426). In *Scientology: The Fundamentals of Thought* (1956) and thereafter, "clear" was no longer defined simply as the optimization of mind and abilities but as "a thetan who can be at cause knowingly and at will over mental matter, energy, space, and time as regards the first dynamic (survival for self)."[24] The concept "thetan" no longer refers to a mental state but is analogous to the Christian concept of "spirit" or "soul" which is immortal and is above both brain and mind. Secondly, the notion of "engram" chains was extended beyond the foetal state to include "past lives and past deaths." In *Science and Survival* (1951), Hubbard, voicing his wariness of "spiritualism," nonetheless cautioned auditors not to "invalidate" evidence for past lives and past deaths showing up in the auditing sessions. Thirdly, the four dynamics of the Dianetics phase were augmented to include "animal," "universe," "spirit" (thetan), and "Infinity" or "God."[25] Fourthly, there was the introduction of the "E-meter" into the auditing session. Due to a court case, the church places a qualification on the use of the E-meter: "The E-meter is not intended or effective for diagnosis, treatment or prevention of disease."[26] From the perspective I am suggesting, however, the use of the E-meter is better seen as a "technological sacrament." Just as Christians define a sacrament (e.g., baptism) as an "outward or visible sign of inward or invisible grace," so Scientologists see the E-meter as an external or visible indicator of an internal or invisible state ("clear").

The four factors which demarcate the transition from Dianetics to Scientology changed the fundamental character of the therapeutic sequence. No longer was the goal simply to get "clear" but also to become an Operating Thetan ("OT"). Thus, the Gradation Chart was expanded to include levels both for pre-clear to clear, and for post-clear (Operating Thetan) and beyond. The introduction of the notions of past lives/deaths and "thetan" caused considerable dissension within the movement between those who wanted to retain the more empirical base of the earlier Dianetics and those who wanted to be more open to spiritual implications of the movement. The essential differences between Dianetics and Scientology can be summarized in the following diagram.

	THERAPEUTIC SEQUENCE			DYNAMICS
DIANETICS	pre-clear foetal engrams	auditing verbal only	clear	self sex group Mankind
SCIENTOLOGY	pre-clear past life/ death engrams	auditing verbal + E-meter	clear + Operating Thetan	4 above + animal universe spirit Infinity/ God

After the development of the ideas specific to Scientology proper, the movement gradually assumed more characteristics of what is classically known as a "church." First and foremost was the centralization of authority in Hubbard and the Executive Council Worldwide and the development of an ecclesiastical policy. The relation between Hubbard and the Executive Council Worldwide looks remarkably like the relation between the Pope and the Roman Curia or between a bishop and his chancery. The policy statements, which are in a state of evolution, also remind one of Canon Law. Finally, there was also the formalization of a Creed, the introduction of religious ceremonials for "naming," marriage and burial, and the appointment of ministers.

The evolution of Dianetics into Scientology is both continuous and discontinuous. On one hand, in the church's current self-understanding, Dianetics remains a "substudy" of Scientology and is used for "Dianetic Pastoral Counselling.''[27] Likewise, Hubbard introduced the notion of ''theta'' energy as a ''postulate'' to explain what he believed to be empirical and experimental evidence.[28] On the other hand, the notion of past lives/deaths and Operating Thetan, the use of the E-meter, the addition of new ''dynamics,'' the centralization of authority, are not continuous with what had gone on before. Whatever else may be said about the transition from Dianetics to Scientology, it is quite true that Dianetics promised ''trans-normal'' rewards to its adherents, whereas Scientology is now promising ''transcendental,'' ''supra-natural'' rewards to its believers: total freedom, complete knowingness, the meaning of life and death, the meaning of the universe.

Scientology's Self-understanding: Seven Characteristics

In this section I discuss seven characteristics which are central to Scientology's self-understanding. These characteristics can be compared and contrasted to notions which inform the traditional religious consciousness of the West. The characteristics also tell us something about Scientology as a fusion of technology and Buddhism.

(1) *Research vs. Revelation.* Religions like Judaism and Christianity approach the dimension of the sacred ''from the top down.'' The Sacred is believed to come to humans in an external revelation (e.g., Moses and the burning bush) which is delivered from ''above'' and which is then codified into a sacred scripture. Other religious traditions, however, approach the dimension of the sacred ''from the bottom up'' or ''from the inward to the outward.'' Instead of looking upward for a revelatory experience which is deemed beyond human capacity, this latter type of religion looks inwards for the illumination of the sacred. Both Buddhism and Scientology fall into this second category. There have been examples of the second type within Christianity. Certain Christian groups like the Quakers, which have stressed the doctrine of Glorification/Sanctification (Holy Spirit) over the doctrines

of Creation (Father) and Redemption (Son) have had a tendency to be illuminationist rather than revelationist.

Scientology adds a "scientific" framework to its Buddhistic base. Scientologists universally express the belief that Hubbard's discoveries are founded on "research" even when this means examining religious teachings from other traditions. The research model has allowed the movement to be rather open-ended. This explains, for example, much about the transition from Dianetics to Scientology as well as the seemingly endless subdivision and expansion of the levels of auditing.[29] The research model also reinforces experimental and experiential knowing for oneself. The common expression is: "If it is not true for you, it is not true." There are qualifications to this dictum.

(2) *Standardness vs. Infallibility/Inerrancy.* Although Scientology places a high priority on knowing for oneself, there is one aspect of the religious system which functions as an absolute or near-absolute. That is the "standardness" of "the tech." The standardness of the technology in Scientology can be compared to the doctrine of infallibility of the Pope and *magisterium* in Roman Catholicism and the doctrine of the inerrancy in scripture in certain branches of Protestantism. Whereas infallibility and inerrancy guarantee the content of teaching ("the message"), the doctrine of standardness in technical application guarantees the form of the teaching in Scientology ("the medium").

The doctrine of standardness arose in response to splinter groups and competing "researchers" in the early phases of the movement.[30] In the crucial HCO Policy Letter, dated February 7, 1965, and entitled "Keeping Scientology Working," Hubbard arrogated to himself all the basic discoveries in the technology:

> In all the years I have been engaged in research I have kept my comm lines wide open for research data. I once had the idea that a group could evolve the truth. A third of a century has thoroughly disabused me of that idea. Willing as I was to

accept suggestions and data, only a handful of suggestions (less than twenty) had long run value and *none* were major or basic; and when I did accept major or basic suggestions and used them, we went astray and I repented and eventually had to "eat crow."[31]

Today, when a question about the technology arises in auditing situations, individuals are discouraged from giving their own interpretation. Instead members are required to check out in the technical manuals any subject which has come under question. Thus "standardness" is preserved. It may be assumed that after Hubbard's death "the tech" will assume canonical status. The control which Hubbard has exerted over the standardness of "the tech" can be compared with the efforts of sectarian leaders to maintain control over the printed word in order to hold in check the centrifugal forces which the spread of a movement sets into play.

(3) *Knowingness vs. Faith/Reason.* In the Western religious heritage there has always been a tension, and sometimes actual conflict, between faith and reason, or between the revealed will of God and what mankind can know on its own. In particular, Christianity has stressed that salvation does not come through knowledge but through faith. In Scientology this tension or conflict does not form a part of the self-understanding of the adherents. Scientology defines itself as a "knowing how to know." "Knowingness" or "self-determined knowledge" is a comprehensive concept embracing what outsiders would distinguish as matters of faith and matters of knowledge.[32] Thus, Scientology includes within the notion of "knowingness" the knowledge of both spiritual and material things.

The self-understanding of Scientology as a *science* causes not a little confusion. In the culture at large, the term "science" is limited to knowledge which results from the observation of an experimentation with quantifiable material phenomena. However, we may note that the medieval theologians called theology the *scientia divina* or *scientia sacra* and even today the French refer to *les sciences religieuses*. Secondly, in North American religious circles, the self-interpretation of belief has had both an experiential and scientific coloring which dates from the Puritan conception of theology as *technologia*. Mary Baker Eddy, for example, called her principal theological treatise *The Science of Health: With a Key to the Scriptures*. Even the hermeneutics of the turn-of-the-century evangelical dispensationalists grounded itself on Scottish Common Sense and "a Baconian system, which first gathers the teachings of the word of God, and then seeks to deduce some general laws upon which the facts can be arranged."[33] Finally, Christians would tend to classify Scientology as a species of "gnosticism" or doctrine that "salvation comes through knowledge." Scientology, however, does not use the term "salvation" but "survival."

(4) *Engrams vs. Sin.* Scientologists make a distinction between reactive mind and analytical mind. The reactive mind, roughly equivalent to the unconscious, records "engrams" or traces of pain, injury or impact.[34] Engrams are unconscious "mental image pictures" which result from traumas extending back to the foetal state and even to "past lives." Unless one is freed from these entangling engrams through the re-stimulation of the analytical mind, (roughly, equivalent to consciousness) a person's survival ability, happiness and intelligence, are considered to be severely impaired. Engrams are discovered and eradicated through the techniques of the dianetic auditing process. Someone freed from all engrams is called a "clear." There are now levels of auditing for "post-clears" or "Operating Thetans." The level "clear" promises ability to be at cause over only the First Dynamic (survival for self), but level OT VI and above, for example, promise "power on all 8 dynamics."[35]

The sequence engrams/clear (and beyond) can be compared to the Christian sequence sin/justification, or sin/forgiveness through grace. Consistent with its belief in an external revelation, Christianity maintains that the source of grace must come from outside. Consistent with its Buddhist-like notion of inner enlightenment, Scientology holds each member responsible for the eradication of engrams. Some have claimed that the addition of post-clear levels of enlightenment amounts to a mystification of the notion of clear. This kind of development, however, is not without precedent. St. Bonaventure's *Triplica Via* (threefold way divided into *purgatio, illuminatio,* and *perfectio*) was expanded into *sensatio, imaginatio, ratio, intellectus, intelligentia* and *unio mystica* in his *Itinerarium Mentis in Deum.*

(5) *Organization vs. Charisma.* One of the unique features of Scientology has been the number of organizations which have been developed to apply the technology to areas like education, mental health reform, drug rehabilitation, prison reform.[36] One might even say that it is an organizational religion which meets the perceptions and needs of the organizational person of a mass society. Max Weber tended to see religious evolution as a transition from an original charismatic phase followed by a routinization of the charisma in rules, organizations and specializations.[37] This model of interpretation needs to be modified to account for a phenomenon like Scientology. From one aspect, Hubbard functions as a "charismatic leader" and as the original "researcher." From another aspect, however, the "charismatic message" is the technology itself. It is as if technique and routinization were given charismatic legitimacy.

This aspect of Scientology invites us to rethink the definition of religion. Webster's Dictionary stresses only the system of beliefs, e.g., a belief in the Supreme Being. Other definitions give equal weight to the cultus or rites. Few definitions, however, note the interplay between the belief system, the ritual practices and the organizational association, or congregation, which guarantees the maintenance of the beliefs and practices. The word *religion* is derived from *religare* which means "to bind back together." This leads me to the broad definition of religion as a system of beliefs expressed in symbols which binds together the lives of individuals and/or groups, which issues in a set of religious practices (rituals), and which is sustained by an organized mode of life. The beliefs, practices and mode of life bind together the lives of people so as to give their existence ultimate meaning. While all religions have rudimentary elements of all three aspects, some, for example, stress the organizational system, or mode of life, over the belief system or the ritual practices. In Scientology we see an example of a group that began with religious practices (the auditing techniques), soon developed a strong ecclesiastical structure and only then formalized its belief system into a creed. This does not mean that the belief system was not latent in the earlier phases of the church's evolution. It simply was not codified in a formal manner the way the organizational technology was from the start.

(6) *Technique vs. Ceremony.* The ritual practice centers on the techniques of the auditing process. The church later instituted traditional ceremonies for initiation or christening, marriage and funerals. This may simply be an accommodation to the standard image of religion in North America and the beginnings of an incipient denominalization. By their nature, ceremonies tend to be "world-maintaining," confirmatory of the status quo, and dedicated to preserving tradition. Ritual, on the other hand, is "person-transforming," demarcative not of social states but of social transitions, and open to social innovation.[38] Scientology may be said to have "technological rituals."

In the narrow sense of the term, technique is the purposive-rational application of the empirico-analytic sciences for the sake of acquiring mastery over the external environment. Scientology inverts this understanding of technique and sees it as a symbolic-interpretative model for acquiring mastery over the internal environment of the psychic processes. This internalization of the model of technique seems common in technological civilization. Even "humanistic" management psychologists are now defining human beings as "information processing centers." This certainly illustrates Jacques Ellul's observation that "when technique enters into every area of life, including the human, it ceases to be external to man and becomes his very essence."[39] Many critics of technological consciousness, including Jacques Ellul, see in it the suppression of symbolic interaction in favor of purposive-rational work, the repression of the ethical, and the fettering of free and open communication in favor of technical problem solving. Scientology shares no such fears of technology. Rather, by internalizing and symbolizing the model of technological consciousness, Scientology expects to bring about total communication and total freedom. Whether the technological model ends up confirming or transforming the social status quo remains to be seen, but the aggressiveness and ingenuity with which the church has pursued the Freedom of Information Act, prison reform, and other social ends, certainly speaks for the reformational and transformational role the church chooses for itself.

(7) *Survival vs. Salvation.* In the dominant religious tradition of the West the ultimate future is seen in categories like salvation/damnation or heaven/hell. By contrast Scientology takes a Darwinian view of the ultimate future and speaks of survival/succumbing. The fundamental "dynamics" of all existence are seen in terms of survival.[40] The ultimate benefit of the dianetic auditing process is to give the individual "the highest possible potential of survival." Survival is not limited to the biological survival of the fittest but also embraces survival as spirit ("thetan") and survival to Infinity (the Eighth Dynamic). The emphasis on survival reflects Hubbard's view of the threat posed by World War II. Like many post-war revitalization movements, Scientology looks toward survival in "abundance." The belief in the ultimate survival of humanity rests on a belief in mankind's

basic goodness. The Creed of the church states:

> *And we of the Church believe:*
> That man is basically good.
> That he is seeking to survive.
> That his survival depends upon himself and upon his
>   fellows, and his attainment of brotherhood
>   with the Universe.

The Creed also states that "*the laws of God forbid Man*...to destroy or reduce the survival of one's companion or one's group."

The notion of survival has been raised here to the status of a religious concept. This is no different from the Latin word *salvere,* "to preserve, keep whole," serving as a metaphor for "salvation" in traditional religious imagery. The elevation of the notion of survival also reflects a religious response to the global effect of World War II and the use of the ultimate weapon during that war.

Conclusion

In *The Genealogy of Morals* Nietzsche predicted the coming of a European form of Buddhism which would represent "the beginning of the end, stagnation, nostalgic fatigue, a will that had turned *against* life."[41] In one sense Nietzsche's prediction has been correct. The Western religious tradition has been subjected to the destructive onslaught of critical consciousness—the disenchantment of the world, the decoding of dreams, the demystification of economic forces and the demythologization of the scriptures themselves. One of the consequences of critical consciousness, I think, has been the turning of the twentieth century to the East for the revitalization of religious consciousness. Scientology represents one aspect of this turning to the East. Where Nietzsche's analysis goes awry is his underestimation of the resourcefulness of symbols to give new life and meaning to existence. Scientology's employment of Buddhistic elements has not led to an enervation of the will in a technological civilization but to an investment of technology itself with symbolic power that gives meaning to the believer's existence. Some may think this is "illusion" and others may think that Scientology does not constitute a "new religious molecule" but an unstable "amalgam," yet Scientology stands out among the new religions as the indigenization of Buddhism within a society that has technology as its cultural base.

Hegel was the first to point out that modern religion (the Protestant principle of inwardness) terminated in the Christianizing of the *saeculum* which led to the secularization of Christianity itself.[42] As an example of post-modern religion, Scientology represents the resacralization and remythologization of the *saeculum*. Some may have expected the revitalization of Christianity itself rather than a fusion of Buddhism and technology. Though there are many examples of Christian vitalizing movements, the turn to the East and the investment of egalitarian technologism with mythic meaning may be just an exemplification of H. Richard Niebuhr's acute observation: "In the course of succeeding generations the heritage of faith with which liberalism has started was used up. The liberal children of liberal fathers needed to operate with ever diminishing capital."[43]

NOTES

The following abbreviations for official Scientology publications will be used:

BCS: *The Background and Ceremonies of the Church of Scientology of California, World Wide* (1970).

DMS: *Dianetics: The Modern Science of Mental Health, A Handbook of Dianetic Therapy.* New York: Paperback Library, 1950.

FOT: *Scientology: The Fundamentals of Thought* (1956).

OEC: *The Organization Executive Course: An Encyclopedia of Scientology Policy* (1972 ff.). Volumes 0-6.

SOS: *Science of Survival: Prediction of Human Behavior* (1951).

SWR: *Scientology: A World Religion Emerges in the Space Age* (1974).

WIS: *What is Scientology?* (1978).

1 *WIS*, p. 3.

2 For a creative reinterpretation of the taxonomy, see Roy Wallis, "Yesterday's Children," in Bryan Wilson, ed., *The Social Impact of New Religious Movements* (Barrytown, N.Y.: Unification Theological Seminary, distr. Rose of Sharon Press, 1981), pp. 117-21.

3 Rodney Stark, "Must All Religions Be Supernatural?," in Wilson, p. 168.

4 Demos Shakarian (as told to John and Elizabeth Sherrill), *The Happiest People On Earth* (Old Tappan, N.J.: Spire Books, 1975).

5 See Wallis, p. 119.

6 See my article, "Law, Language and Religion," *New ERA Newsletter*, 1, no. 2 (May-June 1981).

7 See Leo Strauss, *On Tyranny*, Revised and Enlarged (Ithaca: Cornell University Press, 1963), p. 24.

8 Hans-Georg Gadamer, *Truth and Method* (New York: Seabury Press, 1975), pp. 273-74.

9 W. Brede Kristensen, *The Meaning of Religion*, trans. John B. Carman (The Hague: Martinus Nijoff, 1960), p. 7.

10 *WIS*, p. 7.

11 See Heinrich Zimmer, *Philosophies of India*, ed. Joseph Campbell (Princeton: Princeton University Press, 1951), pp. 464-87.

12 *WIS*, p. 332, s.v. "Clear."

13 *BCS*, pp. 13-15.

14 *WIS*, p. 332, s.v. "Clear."

15 *SWR*, pp. 9-10.

16 See George Grant, "The computer does not impose on us the ways it should be used," in *Beyond Industrial Growth*, ed. Abraham Rotstein (Toronto: University of Toronto Press, 1976), pp. 117-31.

17 Perry Miller, *The New England Mind: The Seventeenth Century* (Cambridge, Mass.: Harvard University Press, 1967), p. 166.

18 Francis Bacon, *The New Organon and Related Writings*, ed. Fulton H. Anderson (Indianapolis: Library of Liberal Arts, 1960), p. 25.

19 See George M. Marsden, *Fundamentalism and American Culture* (New York: Oxford University Press, 1980), pp. 55-62.

20 Max Weber, *The Protestant Ethic and the Spirit of Capitalism*, trans. Talcott Parsons (New York: Scribner's, 1958), pp. 98-128.

21 There is renewed interest in healing even within mainline Christianity. See Morton T. Kelsey, *Healing and Christianity In Ancient Thought and ModernTimes* (New York: Harper & Row, 1973).

22 See George Grant, "Conceptions of Health," in *Psychiatry and Responsibility*, ed. Helmut Schoeck and James W. Wiggins (Princeton: Van Nostrand, 1962), pp. 117-34. Grant notes that modern therapies

have a clear conception of disease but an unclear conception of health.

23 In particular, Scientologists are opposed to the stimulus-response conception of man proposed by Wilhelm Wundt. See *WIS*, pp. 97-98.

24 *WIS*, p. 332, s.v. "Clear."

25 Cf. *DMS*, p. 10, and *FOT*, pp. 36-39.

26 See *WIS*, publication page (p. v.).

27 See "To the Reader," *DMS*, p. 2.

28 *SOS*, I:3-5.

29 See *WIS*, pp. 56-65.

30 On the splinter groups, see J. Gordon Melton, *The Encyclopedia of American Religions* (Wilmington: McGrath, 1978), II: 223 ff.; Roy Wallis, *The Road to Total Freedom: A Sociological Analysis of Scientology* (New York: Columbia University Press, 1977), pp. 84 ff.

31 *OEC*, 5: 44.

32 *WIS*, p. 336, *s.v.* "Knowingness" and p. 339, s.v. "Scientology."

33 Arthur T. Pierson, *Addresses on the Second Coming of the Lord: Delivered at the Prophetic Conference, Allegheny, Pa., December 3-5, 1895* (Pittsburgh, 1895), p. 82, quoted in Marsden, p. 55.

34 *WIS*, p. 334, s.v. "Engram(s)."

35 *WIS*, p. 64.

36 See *WIS*, pp. 85-139, for a survey of the organizations initiated by Scientology.

37 Max Weber, *From Max Weber: Essays in Sociology*, trans. and ed. H.H. Gerth and C. Wright Mills (New York: Oxford University Press, 1946), pp. 267, 297.

38 On the distinction between "ceremony" vs. "ritual," see Victor Turner, *The Forest of Symbols: Aspects of Ndembu Ritual* (Ithaca: Cornell University Press, 1970), p. 95.

39 Jacques Ellul, *The Technological Society*, trans. John Wilkinson (New York: Vintage Books, 1964), p. 6.

40 *SOS*, I, pp. x-xi.

41 Friedrich Nietzsche, *The Birth of Tragedy* and *The Genealogy of Morals*, trans. Francis Golffing (New York: Doubleday Anchor Books, 1956), p.154.

42 G.W.F. Hegel, *The Philosophy of History*, trans. J. Sibree (New York: Dover, 1956), pp. 341-46.

43 H. Richard Niebuhr, *The Kingdom of God in America* (New York: Harper Torchbooks, 1959), p. 194.

Part III:
Religious Alternatives

The Many Faces of Krishna

Larry D. Shinn

In reflecting on my recently completed fieldwork among Hare Krishna devotees, two observations stand out boldly in my mind. The first is that the processes of joining and the levels of participation by members are far more complex than is usually recognized by either anti-cult antagonists or academic analysts. This suggests that a multitude of variables must be taken seriously in describing the processes of affiliation among the Hare Krishna. There is no single process, motive, or factor, like "brainwashing" or "alienation," that can explain how and why all new adherents enter and persist in a "new" religious movement like the Hare Krishna movement. The second observation is that the religious, or spiritual, dimensions of joining and participating in a group such as the Hare Krishnas are undervalued, or even ignored, by many secular scholars. This impression argues for investigations of the complex blending of emotion and reason which religious conversion seems to include, and which is not easily quantifiable in social science categories or statistics.[1]

To demonstrate the validity of these two observations, I will describe the sources of this study, the methods of data collection, and then compare my sample of Krishna members with that of Stillson Judah.[2] Then I will discuss briefly how Judah and other researchers interpreted their data. Finally, by comparing the "typical" Krishna devotee with Eileen Barker's "typical" Unificationist,[3] and by narrating in some detail the story of one Krishna member, I attempt to clarify why studies that rely on a single variable or process may be helpful but remain incomplete, and why such a nebulous characteristic as "spiritual/religious" may be a useful and accurate interpretive rubric. In other words, cult members must be taken seriously when they say they are in search of the sacred.[4]

Sources and Methods

The three basic sources of information for this study were personal interviews, participant observation, and available selected literature. I conducted more than ninety interviews with Krishna devotees which ranged from one and a half to eleven hours each, the average length being three hours. These interviews focused on the pertinent pre-Krishna events of the life story and especially on the period between first contacting the movement and actually joining it. These interviews were relatively informal, allowing the member to tell his or her story in a conversational style, yet sufficiently organized to elicit the relevant background information about the individual as well as specific attitudes and experiences of Krishna "consciousness."

More than two dozen interviews provided information peculiar only to members in India and are excluded from the data of this report. For example, some of the Life Members in India were not actually living in temples. Others concentrated on the special problem of whether or not Indian members were ready to accept the recently established International Society for Krishna Consciousness (ISKCON).[5] We were, therefore, asking only American Krishna devotees about the socioeconomic status of their families, their own educational attainments, their religious backgrounds. We asked also about their first and significant contact with the movement, why they made the decision to become a Krishna devotee, and how they interpreted their early experiences within the movement.

A second major aspect of this investigation was participant observation while living in Krishna Temples in Los Angeles and Berkeley (June 29-July 15, 1980), in Bombay and Vrindavana (September 20-October 9, 1980), in Philadelphia, Washington, Atlanta, Miami, Cita Nagari Farm, and New Vrindaban's "Krishna Land" (January 25-February 16, 1981). While staying at these temples I participated in various rituals, observed and filmed first and second initiation ceremonies. I also spent many hours of informal conversations with members of the various Krishna communities, leaders of the movement, and parents of the devotees. To get a broader perspective I also attended anti-cult conferences and interviewed lawyers, psychiatrists and clergymen who represent a broad spectrum of attitudes toward ISKCON and other "new" religious movements.

The third source of my data is the literature authored by scholars in devotional Hindu studies as well as in the publications about "alternative" religions, the books and articles distributed by ISKCON itself, and the popular magazine and newpaper accounts of Krishna and other "cultic" movements. Although I am reporting here only on American Krishna informants, I feel more competent to assess Krishna devotion and religiosity in the Indian context because my own traditional academic training was in South Asian religions, Hinduism and Buddhism. As a historian of religion with a stronger focus on the humanities than on the social sciences, I am not quite comfortable in the camp of sociological and psychological scholars who helped most to develop the study of new religious movements. These potential weaknesses, however, may also offer some strengths in suggesting new analytic models for the understanding of Krishna devotees.

Profile of Respondents

Stillson Judah's book, *Hare Krishna and the Counterculture,* is the best book-length study of American devotees of ISKCON, and we are able to make some comparisons between the sixty-three persons of his sample and the seventy-two members on whom we are reporting in this survey. His study was localized at the Krishna temples in Berkeley and Los Angeles, and conducted during the years 1971-74. There are more similarities than differences between the subject populations of these two studies, but I discuss here the differences as provocative contrasts which help sharpen the research generalizations rather than as arguable and defendable statistical variances of the two studies.

Chronological age was not one of the criteria I used in selecting the sample of devotees to be interviewed. I asked, instead, to speak with people according to their length of involvement in the Krishna movement. This criterion allowed me to distinguish between those (81%) who know the founding guru, Prabhupāda, by whom they were initiated, and those (19%) who were trained by one of the eleven initiating gurus who have taken over the role of spiritual guide for new members since the death of the founder in 1977. I made an effort also to balance the ratio of male and female members, as well as that of institutional leaders and followers.

It should be obvious that the newer devotees in both studies are mainly those in the younger age cohorts. As they grow older they are likely, at least in some cases, to assume positions of leadership in the temple. A significant difference between the two samples is that a much larger proportion of the Judah study (85%) than of the present study (31%) were twenty-five years of age or younger. It was not uncommon in the early 1970s that youngsters in their late teens joined the Krishna movement. This is no longer the case, or it may be a rare exception that a temple accepts members at this tender age. The propaganda distributed by anti-cult groups, the activities of deprogrammers, and the objections of some parents have introduced a certain degree of caution in this regard. The natural concerns of the public relations image of ISKCON have also contributed to a somewhat later age of entrance to the temple.

While I do not have an exact statistic on the average number of years in the movement, it was certainly more than five years among the persons I interviewed. The membership in both of these studies reflect a kind of institutional settling down, an organizational stability as well as less frequent mobility of individuals from one temple to another.

As may be expected in the process of institutionalization some temples and farm communities acquired the reputation for either stability or flux of membership, and this assists the new member to choose a compatible residence more quickly. There are some members who spent their whole time in the movement at New Vrindaban, even while the Chicago temple experienced several major turnovers of membership (the most recent in the fall of 1980).

From the perspective of socioeconomic status the Krishna members of this study are quite similar to those in Judah's study when he says that they "are largely upper middle class."[6] Very few came from economically disadvantaged, while four of the interviewees were clearly from upper-class families, as measured by wealth, style of life, and father's occupation. While the spiral of inflation makes difficult a comparison of shifting annual income, the great majority report that when they joined the movement their family income was about twenty-five thousand dollars a year. A key to the socioeconomic status of these individuals is their general exposure to white-collar and professional occupational spheres, as well as a high level of interest in educational advancement and attainment.

Unlike the elite among the Moonies, who are given the opportunity to pursue graduate studies, the Krishna devotees do not anticipate a further academic or scholarly career. Among the interviewees of this study I found that thirty percent had actually earned a college degree. At the lower educational level were thirty-five percent who had gone no further than high school. This leaves one-third of the members in a middle category of those who had had from one to three years of college. While I did not enquire about the exact scholastic grade averages while they were in school, my impression is that these devotees were probably similar to Judah's statistics which show that well over half of them had academic grades of B or better. For many of them the early involvement with ISKCON was accompanied by an increasing disinterest in school tasks rather than by any lack of intellectual competence. What came through clearly in the interviews was a general image of mentally alert young people.

Family and Religion

While the findings of the Judah study are similar to those of the present investigation in the areas of educational achievement and socioeconomic status, we must report certain dissimilarities in the family situation of devotees and in their religious background. Only one-fourth of Judah's sample said that they had close relations with their parents and expressed a favorable attitude toward the members of their families. The overwhelming majority (75%) of them said there was a lack of mutal respect, little cordial communication and a generally "unfavorable" attitude toward their family relationships.[7] This relatively sharp contrast between favorable and unfavorable categories of respondents did not obtain among the devotees I interviewed.

A small minority (14%) of the persons I interviewed expressed predominantly negative attitudes, lack of respect, poor communication, general dissatisfaction, all of which pointed to a tension-filled or unhappy home life. In the contrasting category, forty percent came from cheerful homes and used words like "very close," "supportive," and "very happy" to describe their family relationships. Another significant minority (36%) fall into a kind of middle category, manifesting essentially neutral attitudes by saying that their home life had been "O.K." or "No problem," or "Just normal, I guess." The remaining minority (10%) had mixed, if not ambivalent, feelings about their family background, like the one who commented that "my father and I were very close, but my mother and I just didn't get along." In other words, such individuals were probably just as willing to leave home as were the 14% minority who had clearly negative attitudes. If we combine these two catego-

ries into one-fourth (24%) who are negative, we may surmise that the remaining three-quarters (76%) were fairly
satisfied with their pre-Krishna home experience. These are
notably and exactly the opposite proportions of favorable
and unfavorable responses told to Stillson Judah.

I would suggest at least two possible avenues of explanation for the contrast in Judah's 1974 and my 1980 groups
of respondents. First of all, the enthusiasm of the new
convert has passed for many of the respondents in my
study. This means that initial excesses of emotion invested
in the new way of life have been tempered over the years as
the maturing faith of the established devotee permits a
reclaiming of old relationships (including family ones) that
were repudiated in the initial appropriation of a new faith
and life. It is not uncommon for respondents to say that
their family's original hostility centering on the decision to
join the Krishna movement has given way to attempts (some
fledgling, others successful) to rebuild relationships. In fact,
there are instances of devotees claiming closer relationships with parents or family members now than before
becoming a member.

In the second place, the Krishna movement itself has
slowly come to the conclusion that the positive effects of
seclusion for a new devotee's fragile faith are more than
undercut by the extremely negative publicity for the movement caused by irate parents, family and ex-members who
charge the movement with breaking up families. The mature devotees reluctantly admit that parental-devotee communications were discouraged up to the early and mid-1970s
depending on location. This policy stemmed from the belief
that one's "associations" are critical to one's life choices
and behavior (hardly a new insight from a social scientific
point of view). As one devotee said, "We all knew that the
world of *samsāra* (enticement to the material life of rebirth)
still had a strong hold on a new devotee, and that parents
would use that attachment to try to get them back." But

with the increase in negative publicity (not to mention the birth of the deprogramming phenomenon and its use of the "anti-parent" rhetoric) the leadership of ISKCON began to encourage continuing contact with one's family. This rather informal change in policy surely altered devotees' ability to think and speak in positive terms about their pre-Krishna family experience. I would suggest that this does represent a change in attitude toward family relationships which reflects both personal and institutional maturation among devotees and ISKCON over the past decade.

In the area of the pre-Krishna religious training and affiliation of devotees, my sampling differs to some extent from Judah's. While it is most likely in the case of this background variable that time and nature of sampling differences render comparison least reliable, the contrasts highlight some important features of both groups. Mainline Protestants constitute a little more than one-third of the members in each of these studies. Only seven percent of my interviewees said that they had no pre-Krishna religious affiliation, while Judah, limiting his enquiry to the Los Angeles and Berkeley areas, reports one-quarter with no previous church membership. A much smaller proportion (7%) of my respondents said that they fit into none of the categories of organized religion. It seems proper to note, however, that some among the large minority (30.5%) of Jews in my survey indicated thay they had practically no religious training and had paid hardly any attention to the Jewish rituals and worship services. On the other hand, only about one out of seven (14.5%) of Judah's respondents said that they were Jewish.

It is an interesting fact that the Krishna movement has attracted higher proportions of Catholics and Jews than the percentages of these religious populations in the American society. One possible explanation for the high representation of these two groups among devotees is the nature and demands of the Krishna faith as practiced in America. As this Hindu missionary movement has matured, more and more stress has been placed on serious study and appropriation of the theology and philosophy which might appeal to those raised in tradition-oriented Catholic or Jewish homes. But while a sense of tradition and a stress on ritual practices may be shared by Catholics and Jews, the religious *content* of those traditions differs markedly. Such differences can be seen in the devotees I interviewed. On the one hand, most devotees raised in a Jewish context saw their decision to join the Krishna movement as a *break* with an ethnic-religious family tradition that knew *no* devotion to a personal God. On the other hand, most of the devotees raised in Catholic homes felt that becoming a Krishna devotee was a *continuation* or deepening of their Catholic faith. One young woman said bluntly, "I am a better Catholic now." Another young woman went to a Catholic Church to get the permission of Jesus before joining the Los Angeles Krishna Temple. When pressed, however, both of these young women admitted that they no longer attend Catholic services and really felt that while Krishna theology included their previous Catholic beliefs it also transcended them. One may surmise that a Catholic feels comfortable with the Krishna stress on formal ritual, use of iconography, hierarchical institutional structure, and private prayer life. These similarities may account for some of the appeal the Hare Krishna movement holds for Catholic youth.

One sociological explanation of the high Jewish representation among the Krishnas is that persons raised in Jewish homes have tended to be fairly well-educated. This prepares them to assume leadership roles in the movement when such positions of responsibility open up. My observations in ten temples and two rural communities support the conclusion that the leadership of ISKCON is disproportionately derived from persons coming from Jewish backgrounds. My sampling included five gurus, three temple presidents, three editors of various ISKCON publications, and two members of the Governing Body Committee. Seven of this group of thirteen leaders are from Jewish lineage.

Two additional factors might help explain the high level of Jewish responsibility and visibility among the Krishna leadership. First, the locations of Prabhupāda's initial preaching were in New York and Los Angeles where Jewish recruits were fairly numerous. These early devotees were at hand as the movement matured and as institutional roles had to be filled. Prabhupāda simply turned to those who were gaining maturity in the Vaisnava faith and who had the skills or interests which matched the tasks to be done. It might simply be the case that the meeting of institutional needs by persons of requisite skills happened *to some extent* as the result of historical and geographical coincidence. A second factor which might account for the persistence of devotees from Jewish background *and* others who hold important positions in ISKCON is the vocational satisfaction derived, and the institutional commitment secured, from these relatively high status roles that would be hard to achieve elsewhere at such an early age. These are but tentative suggestions and at best only a partial explanation for the high proportion of Krishna leadership from Jewish background.

Comparisons with Unificationists

If we dare to speak of a "typical" American Krishna devotee who is a recent recruit we recognize a young adult with some college education and with a greater chance of coming from a Catholic or Jewish background than population statistics might reasonably project. The young member comes from a basically happy and fairly supportive family which is located in the middle or upper-middle class. While offering the same basic profile, Judah's Krishna devotee is less likely to have come from a happy family and is more likely to be consciously a product of the counterculture.[8] In 1974 Judah described the new convert to ISKCON as a young person who grew up dissatisfied with domestic restrictions, alienated from national and patriotic loyalty, seeking for meaning and security and discovering it through a sacralization of countercultural values in Krishna's theological garb.[9]

In the aftermath of the so-called "youth revolt" of the late 1960s, Judah's interpretative framework logically stressed the sociocultural factors contained under the rubric of the counterculture. A more conservative mood has come upon the youth of the nation yet there is a continued youthful attraction to groups like the Hare Krishnas and the Moonies. What came through clearly in nearly all of my interviews was that these people had dabbled in Eastern philosophical and religious writings *before* their first Krishna contact. They tended also to view their spiritual quest in very individualistic terms. One female devotee said: "I just felt I had to find a guru to lead me to God." One youth remarked that "I was searching for answers to questions about the ultimate meaning of my life."[10]

The largest and most thorough research project on British Unificationists was conducted over a period of four years by Eileen Barker, whose profile of the "typical" Moonie may be used as a basis for comparison and generalization. She concludes that "As a group, Moonies tend to be young adults who come from basically secure and comfortable, possibly overprotective, backgrounds. Their parents are likely to have been in positions of responsibility, and it is possible that a tradition of service and the concept of duty will have formed part of the taken-for-granted values of childhood." The author relates this family background to the notion that "the potential Moonie's experience of life may have left him with an aching desire to do something even though he does not know what or how. He is looking for someone to give him the chance to give, for someone to help him help."[11]

There is a striking difference between the Unificationists and the Krishna devotees in their religious expectations and their spiritual values. The Moonies tend to emerge from the traditional Christian orientation where one's love of God leads to an ethic of love for one's neighbor. The obligation to serve humanity is understood in physical as well as spiritual terms. Conversely the Krishna first seeks personal salvation and interprets assistance to humanity in spiritual terms, and this translates into an almost exclusive emphasis on preaching and the distribution of tracts as the critical religious activity. Such a contrast is quite expected if one takes seriously the Hindu negation of the cyclical, physical world (*samsāra*), the stress on the need to liberate the eternal soul (*atman*) from the material body, and the necessary concept of rebirth emerging from these two notions. In other words, while there is a general similarity of socioeconomic status among young people who join the various new religious movements, the content of their childhood training and family experiences may have an influence on their decision to join one specific religious group rather than another.

Barker's study affirms the general socioeconomic profile of my own study, including a high percentage of members coming from happy, secure homes. One may infer that Judah and Daner stress too much negative predispositions, or motivations, in accounting for a devotee's decision to join ISKCON. My interviews and observations point toward a more secure and comfortable set of family relationships which are *temporarily set aside* during an intense period of psychological, social, and religious seeking.[12] In fact, it may be the case that it is precisely the positive family relationships coupled with the privileged social and economic background that serve as a springboard to religious experimentation. The point is simply that both the adolescent rejection of home and family and the religious seeker's role have been at least as security-based and as forward-looking as they have been products of alienation and backward-looking or regressive repudiation.

If we examine the spiritual dimensions of the life experience of these young people during their transitional period of searching we ought to understand why a Krishna devotee would not be a Moonie, and vice versa. The prospective Unificationist has been conditioned through his family experiences to seek a "this-worldly" solution to the problems of life's values and meanings. In contrast, the youth who is attracted to the Krishna movement already has a desire for some "other-worldly" solution for the evils of material and physical existence. We must appreciate that these are not irrational or primarily emotional decisions. An objective appraisal of these contrasting approaches to cult membership suggests that religious conversion is far more rational and content-oriented than most behavioral scientists are willing to admit.[13] It helps to explain why some youths are drawn to ISKCON and others to the Unification Church. While both categories of seekers desire a personal God, to whom they surrender completely, they clearly take different avenues to travel to their God.

The Story of Rama Dasa

Any description of the "typical" religious convert drawn from the composite generalizations in statistical averages necessarily omits the subjective and personal reflections of the individual. While such profiles provide a fairly accurate picture of the young Krishna devotee, they are also incomplete as interpretive devices. The name assigned to Rama Dasa is fictitious to protect the interviewee's anonymity, but this abbreviated narrative is true to life in all essential details.

> My name is Rama Dasa and I was born in Chicago, December 7, 1950. I had two brothers and we lived a comfortable life with my parents in the suburbs. My father was a used car dealer who was only moderately successful in his business. Though we were not wealthy, we were a close family with a strong sense of our Jewish heritage. My parents were not practicing Jews, but I grew up with very

strong pro-Jewish and pro-Israeli feelings. Though I was not trained in a religious or ascetic life, even at a very young age I was inclined toward such a life. For example, I wanted to sit on the floor to eat and when my parents refused, I stood at the table because I didn't want to be too comfortable. I used to hate the sight of meat, fish and eggs and avoided them whenever I could. When my parents forced me to eat meat I usually just threw it back up. I gradually developed the ability to eat meat, but clearly traces of my past lives were already exhibiting themselves. I was attracted to poverty (for myself) and was fanatical about personal cleanliness. For example, I always used water on my toilet paper after using the bathroom and felt dirty when I only could use toilet paper.

I was happy in school, all the way through high school. I was on the honor roll each term, had lots of friends and loved to wrestle. I did smoke pot with my friends by the ninth grade, but just to find the deeper meanings in life, not just to escape. At the end of my sophomore year in high school I hitched to California by myself and slept on the beach. I always had this adventuresome spirit which seemed to be seeking something. When I got back to school that fall I began to wrestle but dislocated my shoulder. I never wrestled again.

After graduation, my family moved to Florida. That summer I took LSD for the first time not only to expand my mind but to seek a spiritual experience. The Vietnam War was raging and as I stood back and viewed my society's material and violent values I came to the startling realization that what I had been brought up to believe wasn't true! I didn't want to find the answer to the truth I was seeking in drugs, so I turned to blues music as a new avenue. Gradually, as I began college that fall, I began to read books on religion. I got straight A's my first year in college but really dived into philosophy the most. On my own I was reading a lot of books on Eastern spirituality and finally was initiated into TM (Transcendental Meditation). I was not satisfied with TM but was convinced that I needed to find a spiritual guide, a guru.

I quit school after that first year and sold my car and flew to Europe. As I progressed on my trip through Europe toward India, I made various vows along the way. When I began the trip, I vowed not to smoke pot anymore. As I hitched through Holland, I was disgusted with all the free sex I saw about me and, after one personal experience, vowed not to have sex anymore. That experience occurred when a young Dutch girl offered me a place to stay one night and then tried to seduce me. I finally had to get out of bed and leave her house to wander the streets the rest of the night to escape her clutches. I finally made it to New Delhi and fell in love with the Indian cow. I thought, "She really *is* your mother!" The next time I ate meat I vomitted, and I vowed never to eat meat again. I went to an International Yoga Conference where the gurus ended up fighting over the microphone to convince the audience their path was the best. Disgusted, I headed north to Hardwar, to the mountains and the Ganges.

Arriving at Hardwar I went on to Rishikesh looking for the ashram (religious retreat) of Sivānanda. I spent several days in each of several ashrams casting my western dress aside and adopting the lungi and chadar (loin cloth and shawl) of the religious ascetic. I began my purification process by sitting beside the Ganges River for eight to ten hours a day. I ate little and just wanted to become pure. I had learned the Hare Krishna mantra among the several mantras (chant or prayer formulas) and would chant that or another mantra for hours on end. I found a large rock in the middle of the river I would wade out to sit upon and did so each day for nearly a month. People who came on pilgrimage to Rishikesh would offer obeisances to me. But I still wanted to find a guru to lead me.

I left the mountains of the north and went to Banares and lived among Sáivite (worshippers of the god Shiva) ascetics there. Then I went to Bodhgaya (place of the Buddha's enlightenment) and lived in a Buddhist temple there. I traveled on to Bombay stopping at ashrams all along the way. But while in Bombay, I saw a sign announcing a Krishna festival and went to the first night's program and heard Prabhupāda speak for the first time. Several devotees descended on me to preach to me at the end of the lecture, but I thought all religious paths led to the same goal, so why follow this Indian guru and his band of American and Indian followers? I was impressed with Prabhupāda's lectures and came back each night that week arriving early so I could sit at the feet of the master. Still, I was taking a Burmese meditation course in Bombay which really held more value for me at that moment, so I didn't go back to the Krishna temple anymore during that stay in Bombay.

I arrived in India in 1970 and had met the Krishna devotees early in my stay that first year. But I continued on nearly two years more traveling from ashram to ashram and guru to guru trying to find one I could surrender to. I met and stayed with most of the gurus famous in the West like Muktananda, Maharishi Mahesh Yogi, and so on. I also met many gurus known only locally or regionally in India and stayed for several months with a Rāma ascetic in a small temple on the banks of the Ganges. One thing I learned from all of this experimenting was that all those whom I encountered as being truly holy men were following a single path. About that time I had arrived in Mathura during the birthday festival of Krishna and walked with some Indian Krishna devotees to Vṛndāvana (birthplace of Krishna). I met Bon Maharaja (a godbrother of Prabhupāda) and got some Krishna scriptures at his retreat center. I was not impressed with his spiritual program (seemed too commercial) and after a bout with typhoid fever just wandered from shrine to shrine in this holy city.

I was deeply impressed with the devotion of these Indian people and was treated like a son by them (by this time I had long matted hair and looked much like any other Indian *sadhu* or seeker). One day a bus load of Krishna devotees arrived with Prabhupāda and I went to their temple grounds to hear him speak again. But when I arrived, Prabhupāda was singing one of the old Bengali devotional songs about Krishna and I was struck by my feeling, "This man *is* truly a pure devotee." I wanted to surrender to him, but was put off by the opulence of his temple and by some of the devotees who were with him. I realized that Prabhupāda was the greatest guru I had ever met. He answered all my questions and everything he said was backed by ancient scriptures. Furthermore, I could see he was a living example of what he taught. Nonetheless, I was hesitant to make such a big step as surrendering to him, so I took my parents up on their offer to return to America since they hadn't seen me in three years.

My appearance blew my parents' minds! I ate only vegetarian food, slept on the concrete floor of the patio, and had no idea of what the issues and topics of conversation they were interested in were all about. I stayed with them only a short time before going to New York to find Prabhupāda. He was just leaving for India in three days and said that if I couldn't return to the Indian Vrndāvana, I should go to America's New Vrindaban. So I did and have been here every since. It took me a full year to decide to accept initiation after I came to New Vrindaban because I just wanted to be sure I was making the right decision.

Interpretive Complexity

How are we to understand the affiliation, or conversion, process of new members of religious movements such as Rama Dasa? One way is to look for common patterns of behavior or history among those who join and by making a psychological or sociological profile that isolates the variables which seem predictive of joining. This is the tact of most social scientific studies of new religious movements. Bromley and Shupe provide a good example of such analysis in their essay: "A Role Theory Approach to Participation in Religious Movements." Their study of a selected group of Moonies reflects the tendency toward single-process explanations in most social scientific studies. They describe, and then refute, what they call "motivational models" of conversion and argue instead for a sociological "role-model" theory.[14] They include under motivational models those which assume "a three-stage sequence in religious affiliation: (1) predisposing conditions, such as needs and motives, of the individuals ..., 2) an exposure to new beliefs which appear to those predisposing needs or motives ..., (3) resulting behavior as a committed member of the group." According to motivational studies, an individual's needs, e.g., for community or for ultimate meaning, predispose him or her to be attracted by the appeals of the religious movement which meets those needs.

It is among motivational model studies that both Judah's and Daner's analyses of the Hare Krishna devotees fit. Explaining the alienation process as one which uproots the seeker from traditional values, institutions and relationships, Judah and Daner see the Hare Krishna movement essentially as the provider of institutional structures (ritual, community, etc.) which meet the existential needs the counterculture aroused or intensified but could not finally meet. Judah summarizes the typical process of conversion of Hare Krishna devotees this way:

> The observed pattern of change in the devotees begins with alienation from and rejection of the established culture and its religious forms. In their search for a new style of life, preconverts then move through the chaotic and confused anti-nomianism of the drug-infused counterculture. After suffering disillusionment, they find an alternative style of life that they believe to be fulfilling, and an authority who gives them a way to sacralize it. [15]

Such a profile seems applicable only *in part* to Rama Dasa's journey toward the Krishna fold. Rama Dasa did share the counterculture's criticism of America's Vietnam War efforts, a repudiation of materialistic lifestyle, and a questioning of superficial relationships with family members and friends. Yet Rama Dasa never entered the heavy drug-use circles; he did not reject family or religious roots in conscious protest of their inadequacies. He was not comfortable with hippie travelers, in fact, he chose most often to go the opposite direction. More to the point, while Rama Dasa was alienated from his cultural and religious roots by the time he left for India, his quest for a spiritual master was not a consequence of a period of countercultural experimentation leading to unresolved tension.

Judah lists a series of factors that he deems instrumental in the youthful quest for spiritual community, but only two of these may be applied even approximately to Rama Dasa's religious pilgrimage. To be sure, Rama Dasa did have needs which are being met by his involvement in the Hare Krishna movement, but most of them are clearly the

consequence of personal feelings and private reflection beginning in early childhood and maturing in adolescence.
They are not the result of adolescent alienation or of countercultural involvement. The intense desire to find a guru only
formally fits the countercultural stereotype since Rama Dasa's
lengthy and systematic search reflects a type of commitment known throughout the ages as spiritual pilgrimage.
When viewed in this light, such a search is at least as much
a positive, life-cycle event as one born of the disillusionment
and alienation that Judah suggests.

The quarrel that Bromley and Shupe have with such
motivational analyses is yet a different one. They accuse the
motivational model theorists of psychological reductionism
and they view conversion "not in terms of individual experience and personal feelings, but rather as socially structured
events arising out of role relationships." Instead of answer-
ing the question of *why* people join religious movements,
Bromley and Shupe tackle the problem of *how*. In this
role-theory approach, it is assumed that stages two and
three of the motivational model are reversed. That is, "that
marginal group behavior precedes belief conversion. In the
role-theory approach, therefore, an individual begins per-
forming in a role as the result of the initial interactive
process between the individual and the group which may or
may not involve attitudinal change."[16]

The role theory of religious commitment presupposes
the essential importance of an interactive process between
the individual and the group. Bromley and Shupe identify
five basic components of this process: (1) predisposing factors,
(2) attraction, (3) incipient involvement, (4) active involvement, and (5) commitment.[17] Without trying to anticipate
exactly how Bromley and Shupe would apply their model to
Rama Dasa's case, it should be clear that Rama Dasa did
accept the role of devotee for nearly a year before finally
committing himself unreservedly to their theology. It should
also be equally apparent that the role he lived out was *not*

shaped as much by the formal Krishna organization as by his three years of living with gurus and other seekers. Furthermore, Rama Dasa refused to adopt the primary symbols of the devotee-role, like the shaven head and ochre robe, for more than a year after moving into the temple, and *until* he was fully committed. It is difficult in Rama Dasa's case to sustain the notion that commitment to ISKCON's theology and lifestyle *grew out of* ''organizational role performance.'' Nonetheless, the role-model theory does cause us to look at dimensions of the joining process in a way different from the motivational model, even if both analyses seem inadequate when applied to the specific conversion history of Rama Dasa.

While the case of Rama Dasa fits quite well the composite profile of Krishna devotees that I summarized earlier, profiles alone do not reveal various shadings of characteristics that each individual description demands. It is one thing to say that nearly all devotees had read, or were infatuated with Eastern religious ideas prior to their first Krishna contact, but quite another to see the traditional *Indian* pattern of spiritual pilgrimage adopted by an American youth. It is accurate to say that Rama Dasa came from a secure and supportive home and still recognize that his religious interests were not being encouraged or developed in that family context. While psychosocial profiles of religious converts, together with single-approach theories of religious conversions, help us to understand the general process of joining new religious movements, they are essentially incomplete when they ignore the complex nuances of the human decision-making processes. The case of Rama Dasa lends itself to so many avenues of explanation, that one should be wary of forcing a general profile, or a single explanation, upon his life and decision. For in my lengthy conversation with Rama Dasa, it was clear to me that the highly publicized counter-culture just happened to be in vogue while he was on religious pilgrimage. He never really fit either into his natal, secularized Jewish context or into the counterculture's alternatives. More importantly, rational-emotional and psychological-social processes were always interdependent in the predispositions and roles Rama Dasa acquired at various times in his life. This was especially true during the more than three years of his spiritual odyssey culminating in his decision to accept Prabhupāda's initiation.

What is the spiritual or religious dimension of which I have been speaking throughout this paper? It is none other than the experience of a *relationship* with a sacred power, in this case, Krishna. Rama Dasa moved into the temple because he felt that Prabhupāda could lead him to a personal relationship with God, but it was only after experiencing the presence of Krishna in his extremely rigorous devotional life, however, that Rama Dasa became fully committed. Being quite independent before and after joining the Krishna movement, Rama Dasa was not simply looking for a community. As one who has always had reservations about the material world, it was not just his parents' and society's values he rejected, but transcendent or eternal values he longed for. Most importantly, his spiritual quest was experienced not as an alienation or flight *from*, but as a journey *towards*.[18] These are the nuances that are not reducible to generalized variables or to the "feelings of transcendence" common to institutionalized ecstatic experience.[19]

Elsewhere I have argued that social and psychological processes are reciprocating and interdependent in the founding of religious traditions and in subsequent conversions to them.[20] I am drawn, therefore, to analyses which take into account social and psychological processes of conversion without reducing *all* such experiences to one process alone (e.g., social affiliation) or even to a combination of processes. It may be true that some devotees' affiliation may be *best* understood in motivational and depth-psychological categories, while the conversion of others fits well into the social process model described by Bromley and Shupe, but Rama Dasa's life and decision can be only partially understood by either approach.

After a year of living with Krishna devotees I am impressed with both the variety and the similarity of motives and forces which have led various members to the Krishna movement, but I am even more struck by the instances of genuine religious searching that blend similar social, rational, and emotional experiences in ever new ways.

NOTES

1 See Joseph H. Fichter, "Sociological Measurement of Religiosity," *Review of Religious Research,* 10, no. 3 (1969): 169-76.

2 J. Stillson Judah, *Hare Krishna and the Counterculture* (New York: Wiley & Sons, 1974). For further comparisons see Francine J. Daner, *The American Children of Krishna* (New York: Holt, Rinehart, and Winston, 1976).

3 Eileen Barker, "Who'd Be A Moonie? A Comparative Study of Those Who Join the Unification Church in Britain," in Bryan Wilson, ed., *The Social Impact of New Religious Movements* (Barrytown, N.Y.: Unification Theological Seminary, distr. Rose of Sharon Press, 1981), pp. 59-96.

4 See Joseph H. Fichter, "Youth in Search of the Sacred," in Wilson, pp. 21-41.

5 ISKCON was founded in New York City in 1966 by A.C. Bhaktivedanta Swami Prabhupāda, whose picture appears opposite p. xvi of the Preface to his book, *Śrīmad Bhāgavatam* (Los Angeles: Bhaktivedanta Book Trust, 1972).

6 Judah, p. 111.

7 *Ibid.,* p. 126.

8 This point is made also by Francine J. Daner, "Conversion to Krishna Consciousness: The Transformation from Hippie to Religious Ascetic," in Roy Wallis, ed., *Sectarianism* (New York: Wiley & Sons, 1975), pp. 53-69.

9 Judah, pp. 159-81.

10 The search for a "greater vision" is similarly discussed by Richard DeMaria, "A Psycho-Social Analysis of Religious Conversion," in M. Darrol Bryant and Herbert Richardson, eds., *A Time for Consideration: A Scholarly Appraisal of the Unification Church* (New York: Edwin

Mellen, 1978), pp. 82-130.

11 Barker.

12 Note Barker, p. 85, and Judah, pp.160-62.

13 See the discussion by Thomas McGowan, ''Conversion and Human Development,'' in Herbert Richardson, ed., *New Religions and Mental Health* (New York: Edwin Mellen, 1980), pp. 127-73.

14 David Bromley and Anson Shupe, ''Just a Few Years Seem Like a Lifetime: A Role Theory Approach to Participation in Religious Movements,'' in Louis Kriesberg, ed., *Research in Social Movements: Conflict and Change* (Greenwich: JAI Press, 1979), pp. 159-85.

15 Judah, p. 181.

16 Bromley and Shupe, p. 162.

17 *Ibid.*, p. 167.

18 ''Any religious search is man's attempt to restore the original relationship of love with God,'' Young Oon Kim, *Unification Theology and Christian Thought* (New York: Golden Gate, 1976), p. 40.

19 Judah, p. 4.

20 Larry D. Shinn, *Two Sacred Worlds: Experience and Structure in the World's Religions* (Nashville: Abingdon, 1977).

Catholic Traditionalist Movement

William D. Dinges

Many of the contemporary religious movements in American society, especially those of Eastern derivation, have been called expressions of religious innovation.[1] Catholic Traditionalism is not of this nature; it brings no new *Weltanschauung* to the American religious landscape. Unlike the Charismatic Movement within the Catholic Church, Traditionalists are not motivated by a new theological paradigm intended to revitalize the faith. Instead, Catholic Traditionalism is best understood as a social movement of clergy and laity who are striving to arrest and reverse social change in the church and preserve the religious, ideological, organizational and ritual patterns that have lost much of their institutional legitimacy in the postconciliar church. In this sense it is not only an alternative religious system for dissatisfied Catholics, it is also a demonstration that a social movement need not strive for progressive social reform.[2]

Catholic Traditionalism is a social reaction to the humanistic, horizontally-oriented, world view construction that had gained ascendency in the Roman Church. The movement is a collective protest against the blurring of Catholic identity, against the ''modernist'' transformation of Catholicism, against the demise of religious patterns, values, symbols, and norms that have been abandoned or deprecated as obsolete in the postconciliar era. The movement can be understood in a psychological vein as an adaptive response on the part of some Catholics to the spiritual and structural anomie that has beset contemporary Catholicism. As a sociological phenomenon, the traditionalist movement can be viewed as a separatist alternative of the type long associated with Protestant sectarianism. Finally, Catholic Traditionalism may be recognized as one element in a mosaic of religiously inspired social movements that have risen in the Catholic Church as a consequence of the ideological and organizational vacuum that followed Vatican II.

The Underground Church

It was not uncommon shortly after the Second Vatican Council (1962-1965) to read of the emergence of an "underground church" in America.[3] Among Catholics, the term referred to small groups of liberal laity and priests who met privately in homes and other unofficial locations to celebrate in an unauthorized manner the most ancient of the church's public rituals, the Mass. Priests shed their usual liturgical vestments and dispensed with the traditional rubrics. The use of the vernacular, folk music, and communal type prayers in these small informal gatherings created a new sense of devotional élan unknown to most Catholics up to this time. The participants in this "underground church" were among the first signs that the "Spirit of Vatican II," an ideological leaven popular among progressive Catholics, had begun to ferment.

The term, "underground church," proved short-lived among American Catholics. Within four years after the Council, the Magisterium had officially incorporated a series of wide-ranging changes into the liturgical life of the church, culminating in 1969 with Pope Paul VI's promulgation of a new rite of the Mass (*Novus Ordo Missae*). This new *Ordo* was simplified, vernacularized, and far more participatory in character than the Mass officially approved by the Council of Trent in 1562. The role of the laity was greatly expanded, while the mystique surrounding the cultus of the priesthood underwent a significant transformation in the priest's new role as presiding minister.[4] By the time the implementation of the new *Ordo* became mandatory in 1971, it was clear that many of the innovations of the underground church had been incorporated into the official liturgical life of the official church.

A decade after Vatican II, one could again speak of an "underground church" among American Catholics. This time, however, the term had an entirely different referent. The new "underground church" of the 1970s consisted of a small but growing and dedicated group of self-proclaimed "Traditionalist Roman Catholics" whose far-flung rebel congregations were clinging tenaciously to what they believed to be the essence of the true Roman Catholic faith: the centuries-old Latin Tridentine Mass. As had been the case with the liberal "underground church," Traditionalist Catholics gathered privately in homes, hotel rooms, meeting halls, and *ex officio* chapels. They did not do so, however, to experiment with new liturgical forms, but to preserve the substance of the old. They quietly gathered to hear a cultic ritual that, after 450 years tenure as the central expression of Catholic devotional piety, had been abrogated and replaced by a new rite of worship. Six years after the Second Vatican Council ended, the Mass that all Roman Rite Catholics were bound under pain of sin to attend since the sixteenth century no longer enjoyed the official sanction of the hierarchy. It had been revised in accordance with the mandate of *Sacrosanctum Concilium,* the Vatican II Constitution on the Sacred Liturgy.

Catholics who clung to the old liturgy were accused of being disobedient and were told by their bishops that they were "no longer fulfilling their obligations as Catholics" by attending the Tridentine Mass. In the words of Pope Paul VI, they were "outside obedience and communion with the Successor of Peter and, therefore, outside the church."[5] Within a few years of Vatican II, the question of "Which rite is right?" had been transformed into a more pressing issue involving a crisis of schism and authority. While Traditionalist Catholics circulated polemical literature attacking the new *Ordo* as an "invalid rite," denouncing Vatican II as a "false council," charging Pope Paul VI with apostasy, and asserting that the church had been "infiltrated" by Masons, Communists, and other historic "enemies," official church leaders and Conservative Cathoic apologists warned Catholics of the grave dangers implicit in the Traditionalist Movement.

When the liberal "underground church" emerged in the mid-1960s, one sympathetic commentator argued that the movement's most outstanding characteristic was the participant's disregard for traditional church authority.[6] Just how far that authority has been eroded in the postconciliar church is nowhere more evident than in the rise of the Catholic Traditionalist Movement. The attack on the authority structure of the church is no longer confined to the liberal or progressive wing, but now stems increasingly from a segment of the Catholic population allegedly committed to orthodoxy and the traditional vision of the faith. While many liberal Catholics have apostatized in the last two decades or simply "redefined" Catholicism to fit their own personal preferences in doctrinal or moral matters,[7] the Catholic Traditionalist Movement embodies an organized and institutionalized challenge to the Magisterium of the church predicated on the claim to be the true "remnant Catholic Church."

Conservative vs. Traditional

Before discussing elements of Catholic Traditionalism as a social protest movement and as an alternative form of Catholicism, I want to emphasize that religious conservatives are not synonymous with religious traditionalists. While the popular media image of Catholic Traditionalists focuses on the dispute over liturgical reform and over the preservation of the Latin Tridentine Mass, the character and motivation of the participants are far more complex and variegated.

In order to understand the emergence and appeal of the Catholic Traditionalist Movement, it is helpful to describe briefly how Conservative Catholics, in general, responded to *aggiornamento*—the renewal and updating of the church—since Traditionalism is rooted in this reaction, and cannot be treated in isolation from it. Conservative and Traditionalist Catholics share many of the same anxieties and concerns over the pace and direction of change effectuated in the postconciliar church under the rhetoric of renewal.[8]

Their ideological posture is similar in a number of respects. Both groups have assailed the "neo-modernists" for wrecking the church in a misguided effort to make her relevant to the modern ethos. Both bemoan the weakening of church discipline and doctrine and have argued that *aggiornamento* wedded Catholicism to a *Weltanschauung* fundamentally inimical to Her character. Apologists for both groups have vociferously attacked the desacralization and "destruction" of the liturgy.[9] These ideological affinities notwithstanding, Conservative and Traditionalist Catholics represent two distinct types of social movements in the postconciliar church and differ in distinct ways. Indeed, the hostility between Conservative and Traditionalist Catholics has often been as acrimonious and bitter as that between Traditionalists and the establishment church.

Neil Smelser's distinction between norm-oriented and value-oriented social movements is a useful conceptual means for differentiating between Catholic Conservatives and Traditionalists. He points out that generally different types of reform movements arise during periods of intensified social and cultural strain.[10] Norm-oriented movements seem ready to shift towards more acceptable standards of behavior, which is the case with conservative Catholics. Value-oriented movements are more comprehensive in their outlook. Participants seek to reconstitute, or reestablish, fundamental values that have lost societal legitimacy. Thus, the traditional ideology is more radical in character, both in the diagnosis of the social situation and in the strategies and tactics employed for the resolution of tension. Typically, value-oriented religious movements tend to splinter off from the parent church, as has been the case with rigidly fundamentalist sectarians.

If we apply this value-oriented concept to Catholic Traditionalism, the movement can be understood as an attempt to restore and regenerate many religious and social values that were once prominent in the preconciliar church—

doctrinal certitude, clerical elitism, liturgical uniformity, institutionalized authoritarianism, and an other-worldly religious orientation. Catholic Traditionalists are separatist in their repudiation of the authority of the established church hierarchy. They reject the mandates of the Second Vatican Council and are particularly categorical in their resistance to the *Novus Ordo* liturgy, a ritual they associate with a "Protestant" and humanistic vision of Catholicism.[11]

In their interpretation of the tensions and crises in the contemporary church, Traditionalist Catholics often manifest a near-paranoid and eschatological mind-set, believing as many do that we are now in the time of the "Great Apostasy" foretold by St. Paul in his second letter to the Thessalonians. In the Traditionalist perspective, the dramatic changes in Catholic institutional structures, theological interpretations, and self-understanding, are far too comprehensive and alien to the historical character of the church to be explained as the normal product of social change, or of the development of doctrine. In their minds instead, the complexity of the transformation of Catholicism into a modern idiom is reduced to a category of conspiracy and is interpreted as a vast and sinister plot to obliterate the Catholic faith.[12]

Conservative norm-oriented movements in contrast do not envision an infusion of new values or, necessarily, a return to old ones. Participants are not primarily concerned with bringing about a major orientation in cultural values. They focus rather on specific issues and seek to reinforce normative behavior that is threatened or in need of reform.[13] While I certainly do not mean to imply that all conservative Catholics have readily accepted the new value orientations stemming from Vatican II, neither have they repudiated initiatives to update the church as have most Traditionalist Catholics. Conservative Catholics have instead worked to maintain a normative, strict-constructionist interpretation of what is proper and appropriate *aggiornamento* in the context of the historical discipline and orthodoxy of the church.

With respect to the liturgy, Conservative Catholics have accepted the validity of the *Novus Ordo* rite, but in the face of the thoroughly vernacularized liturgy in the United States they have continued to protest that the conciliar constitution did say that "the use of the Latin language is to be preserved in the Latin rite."[14] On the basis of this statement they correctly argue that the Fathers of Vatican II in no way intended the complete demise of the Latin language in the liturgical life of the church. Rather than reject the authority of the Magisterium, Conservative Catholics seek to uphold that authority against the influence of liberal theologians and intellectuals on the left, and against the programs of the extreme reactionaries embodied in the Traditionalist Movement on the Catholic right.[15] This support has been particularly strong as a hardened defense of papal authority. While Conservatives are generally supportive of American bishops, they do not hesitate to excoriate those prelates who demonstrate liberal social proclivities, or those who have been "lax" with respect to legitimate liturgical innovation or to the teaching of "unsound doctrine" in their diocese.

From the perspective of organized alternative religious movements the critical distinction between Traditionalist and Conservative Catholics is the manner in which the former have embarked upon a course of action—establishing *ex officio* parishes, chapels, seminaries, and other organizational structures—in clear defiance of the ecclesiastical authority of the Pope and the hierarchy of the church, and have thereby placed themselves under the specter of schism.

Organized Forms of Traditionalism

At the present time, there are four major Traditionalist organizations operative in the United States. Within a year after the publications of the conciliar document on the liturgy, Gommar De Pauw, professor of theology and Canon Law at Mount St. Mary's Seminary in Emmitsburg, Maryland, released his own document, the *Catholic Traditionalist Manifesto*. Ideologically mild in tone, this document warned against the danger of stripping Catholics of their traditional patterns of identity, and made a strong appeal for the retention of the Latin liturgy. In December, 1964, he launched the Catholic Traditionalist Movement, Inc., and almost immediately became involved in a canonical imbroglio with his ecclesiastical superior, Cardinal Lawrence Shehan, over his legal standing in the archdiocese (from which he is still listed as "absent" in the 1981 *Official Catholic Directory*). Soon thereafter he moved the headquarters of his Movement to Westbury, New York, from which he continues his activities today.

Although Father De Pauw was the first to attempt to mobilize American sentiments against the "liberal" thrust of the Second Vatican Council, another organization, the Orthodox Roman Catholic Movement, established in 1973 by Francis Fenton and two lay Catholics was the first Traditionalist group to achieve a degree of national organizational stature. This Connecticut priest, who is "absent on leave" from his Bridgeport diocese, had gained attention as a member of the Board of Directors of the John Birch Society and was an active speaker on the organization's national lecture circuit. These connections proved invaluable in establishing a network of sub-groups across the country. At the peak of its growth, in 1979, the Orthodox Roman Catholic Movement counted twelve priest members who worked out of twenty-seven chapels. In that same year, however, there occurred a split in the organization as a consequence of internal factionalism accompanying personality conflicts, overstretched resources, and a power struggle within the leadership. Father Fenton and a small group of his clergy supporters broke away to form the third Traditionalist Movement with a new name, the Traditional Catholics of America, with headquarters in Colorado Springs, Colorado. Meanwhile, the second group, the original Orthodox Roman Catholic

Movement, continues its operations from Monroe, Connecticut, and retains control over those chapels served by Traditionalist priests who remain loyal to it.

The largest and best known Traditionalist organization is the Society of St. Pius X, a religious order founded in 1970 by French Archbishop Marcel Lefebvre. Unlike the previously mentioned organizations, the Society is a priestly fraternity and an international association. Archbishop Lefebvre began the Society of St. Pius X (and established his seminary at Econe, Switzerland) as a means of ensuring a supply of Thomistic-trained priests who would uphold the traditional faith by offering the Latin Tridentine Mass and by administering sacraments in the traditional manner. These goals were integrated into the seminary training program at Econe, which formalized the Archbishop's general repudiation of the documents and decrees of Vatican II.

Lefebvre's serious discord with the Vatican began in 1974 when a canonical investigation (officially designated a "visitation") led to the withdrawal of approval of his "wildcat" seminary as the result of an acerbic "Declaration" issued by Lefebvre in the wake of the visit. On June 29, 1976, in public defiance of an explicit papal directive, Lefebvre ordained thirteen Econe seminarians despite a last-minute appeal by a Vatican Emissary to stop the ordinations. Two days after the ceremony, the Vatican suspended him from conferring orders. On July 22, 1976, he was suspended *a divinis*—an order depriving him of the canonical authority to exercise his priestly powers.[16] Two years before this action, in 1974, the first of Archbishop Lefebvre's Traditionalist priests began establishing chapels and "Mass centers" in the United States. Capitalizing on the visibility the Traditionalist Movement had achieved by this time, and legitimating their activities under an umbrella of ecclesiastical authority (a bona fide religious order headed by an Archbishop), Lefebvre's priests made rapid progress in establishing a national chain of chapels (nearly eighty by 1980), including several

Traditionalist Catholic boarding schools run under the auspices of the Society.

These four identifiable and formally established groups publish their own Traditionalist literature in the form of magazines or newsletters. There are two Traditionalist Catholic papers in the United States: *The Remnant,* begun in December, 1967, by Walter Matt of St. Paul, Minnesota; and *The Voice,* a now defunct paper published between 1967 and 1978 by Hugh McGovern of Canandaigua, New York. There is also a vast body of Traditionalist Catholic literature in the form of books, pamphlets, tracts and periodicals published by self-proclaimed ''lay theologians'' and other Traditionalists unaffiliated with any organization. These publications have played a germinal role in articulating Traditionalist ideology and mobilizing resources on behalf of the Traditionalist cause. Their importance in this regard is especially critical given the virtual blackout of Traditionalist views in the conventional Catholic media.

It is difficult to determine the exact number of Traditionalist Catholics in the United States. Based on the number of subscriptions to Traditionalist publications, attendance rates at Traditionalist chapels, and impressionistic accounts, one may estimate between ten to fifteen thousand Catholics active in the movement. Those are the people who attend the Tridentine Mass on a regular basis and contribute materially to the support of Traditionalist priests, chapels, and schools. Aside from the Catholic Traditionalist Movement, Inc., the Orthodox Roman Catholic Movement, the Catholic Traditionalists of America, and the Society of St. Pius X, there are numerous *ad hoc* Traditionalist flocks scattered throughout the United States.

The 1981 edition of the *Catholic Traditionalist Directory* published by Professor Radko Jansky of Maryville College in St. Louis, Missouri, lists over 250 locations in the United States where the Tridentine Latin Mass is celebrated on a regular basis.[17] It is estimated that more than fifty

Catholic elementary and secondary schools operate under the auspices of Traditionalist teachers and administrators. About ninety Catholic priests identify themselves among the active Traditionalist American clergy, but only one third of them are directly affiliated with any of the four branches of the Traditionalist Movement. Some of the priests are unwilling to make a serious public commitment to the Society of St. Pius X, or to be too openly defiant of their own church superiors. Consequently, they quietly arrange to administer the sacraments in the traditional formula and to celebrate the Tridentine Mass for local congregations that number from a few dozen to over one thousand communicants.

Ideological Themes

Catholic Traditionalists may trace their mind-set back to a solid base of religious conservatism, to the philosophy that applauded Pope Pius X's condemnation of the Modernists, and more recently to the general conservative distaste for the innovations of Vatican II. For a better understanding of the current radicalized Traditionalist perspective it is helpful to review the several ideological positions from which it emerged. Certain central themes underlie the conservative Catholic anxiety over the pace and direction of the conciliar *aggiornamento.*

The first of these was the suspicion that Modernism had again surfaced in the church, and this time at Rome itself, the very citadel of impregnable orthodox Christianity. For more than a century and a half the Vatican had steadily inveighed against the hydra-headed monster of Modernism. Now it appeared that the bishop delegates to the Vatican Council with their liberal theologians and *periti* had insidiously, or ignorantly, reintroduced frequently condemned Protestant errors. It was felt that the documents themselves of Vatican II were often ambiguously worded and sometimes even a contradiction to previous church teachings.[18] Works like Wiltgen's *The Rhine Flows into the Tiber* lent added credibility to the conservative conviction that a modernist-inspired conspiracy was intent on wrecking the bark of Peter on the shoals of *aggiornamento*.[19]

Traditionalist Catholics go one step further than these conservative fears, and the conspiracy theory deepens. To their mind the products of the Council reforms were not simply the work of misguided liberals or modernist theologians and periti; they were the conscious efforts of a full-fledged conspiracy (variously identified as "Satanic-occult," "Jewish-Masonic," "Communist") against the church. To the Traditionalist Catholic, the "battle for the American Church" has a cosmic, eschatological meaning that transcends the secularist understanding of inevitable organizational tensions associated with social change.

A second Conservative Catholic ideological theme concerns the charge that *aggiornamento* is elitist in character and leads to a usurpation of hierarchical authority. As the infra-structure of the Catholic Church underwent further bureaucratization by experts, specialists, and administrative staffs in an effort to "democratize" postconciliar Catholicism, bishops allegedly lost greater amounts of their administrative authority in virtually all church related matters. Professor James Hitchcock, a Conservative Catholic apologist at St. Louis University, summarized the negative character of this new "dominance of expertise" in the postconciliar church:

> Many bishops have had impressed upon them, over and over again, that they are not theologians, not liturgists, not educators, not canon lawyers, and that they are consequently not competent to lay down policy in the various areas of church life. The bishop's role is one of ratifying what bureaucrats do and defending them from the criticism of irate lay people.[20]

While Conservatives generally hold that the bishops have been outbureaucratized or outmaneuvered by progressives, Traditionalists are more blunt and accusatory in charging that the hierarchy has deliberately capitulated to these elements, thereby abrogating their right to speak in the name of the church. This position has obvious utility in legitimating Traditionalist defiance of church authority, since the bishops are not perceived as victims, but rather as culprits in the crisis of contemporary Catholicism.

A third ideological motif prominent in Conservative Catholic quarters concerns the renewal of the liturgy and the conviction that the transformation of the prayer life of the church (which was also allegedly imposed by bureaucratic elites, i.e., "liturgical experts") has seriously weakened the Catholic faith. The dramatic decline in Mass attendance and the demise of traditional devotional practices after Vatican II reinforced these anxieties, and led to an increasingly polemical attack against the new liturgy. It is again indicative of the contrast between Conservative and Traditionalist Catholics that the former have criticized the *Novus Ordo* Mass principally on psychological and aesthetical grounds, while the latter have attacked it as a fundamental doctrinal issue.[21]

Conservatives argue that the new style of the Mass tends to destroy the sense of sacredness and mystery which is fundamental to the Catholic ethos; Traditionalists allege it has been incorrectly translated into the vernacular and is therefore an invalid rite. In the new English translation of the Canon of the Mass, first released in 1967, the phrase "*pro multis*" (for many) had been changed to read "for all men." Traditionalist apologists argued that this alteration in the Canon of the Mass—which, they claimed, clearly violated the strictures of the Council of Trent, the writings of several popes, and the theology of St. Thomas Aquinas— represented an unprecedented tampering with the form of a sacrament and thereby invalidated any rite in which it was used.[22] In this regard, it should be borne in mind that the Traditionalist Catholic commitment to the Tridentine Liturgy is not simply a matter of nostalgic longing or a niggardly resistance to liturgical change (although these issues are involved); it is predicated on the perception that a fundamental error has been introduced into the central ritual/doctrinal expression of Catholicism.

Even a cursory perusal, however, of Conservative Catholic writings of the last two decades leads one to conclude that Catholic Conservatives have only begrudgingly accepted the imposition of the new liturgy. The reason for this acceptance—expressing the norm-oriented character of the Conservative Movement—emerges in part from the turmoil in the church immediately after the Council. By the late 1960s, a clear conviction had arisen among many Conservative Catholics that the dysfunction in the postconciliar church could be directly attributed to the weakening and disregard of church authority. Liberal collisions with the hierarchy over academic freedom, lay autonomy, renewal or religious Orders, a more meaningful voice in ecclesiastical affairs, and the overwhelming negative reaction to *Humanae Vitae* (1968) heightened the perception of a crisis of authority. By the time Pope Paul promulgated the new Mass in 1969, many Conservative Catholics were convinced something had to be done to abate the "schismatic activity" everywhere rampant in the church. If Catholicism was to maintain its institutional and doctrinal integrity, the authority of the pope and bishops had to be upheld—and certainly on an issue as fundamental to Catholicism as the Mass. Support for the *Novus Ordo,* a liturgy clearly mandated by the hierarchy, then became a kind of litmus test indicating one's fidelity to Rome, irrespective of any personal dislike of the new rite.

Role of the Clergy

One of the more intriguing aspects of the difference between Conservative and Traditionalist Catholic movements in the postconciliar church is the fact that while Conservative organizations represent a lay initiative, the Traditionalist

Movement is in its elitist, leadership elements, a clerically inspired phenomenon. Priests are the primary architects of Traditionalist organizations. They occupy the decision-making positions, articulate the dominant motifs in Traditionalist ideology, and play the critical role in mobilizing anti-Vatican II Catholic lay sentiments into an organized social protest movement. While a number of factors may explain their prominence in the movement (the fact that priests have traditionally held the leadership roles in the church), content analysis of Traditionalist literature reveals a conspicuous preoccupation with the status loss in the traditional role identity of the priest. In postconciliar Catholicism, the laity have become—at least in theory—more integrated into the organizational structure of the church. Their involvement in the liturgy, once the exclusive monopoly of the clergy, is now more visible and direct. As a result, the status of the priesthood has shrunk to something of a marginal occupation in which traditional roles and credentials lost their value and appropriateness.[23]

Reaction against the debilitation of the priestly role is especially emphasized in Traditionalist literature and public pronouncements, particularly in regard to criticism of the *Novus Ordo* Mass, since defense of the "true Mass" is implicitly a defense of the traditional role and status of the priesthood. Archbishop Lefebvre, for instance, has repeatedly asserted that the *Novus Ordo* destroys the historic role of the priest as one who "offers sacrifice." According to the Archbishop, this is the priest's principal and fundamental role. However, under the new Mass, "it is no longer the priest who offers the Holy Sacrifice, it is the assembly."[24] Traditionalist lay Catholics who uphold this post-Tridentine priestly status through their adherence to the traditional liturgy and role relations with Traditionalist priests are, collaterally, defending their own religious identity, an identity formed in many cases, in the lay/clerical social dichotomies of the preconciliar church. By implication, the demystification of "Father" has forced an unpleasant rethinking of the religious self-understanding of many lay Catholics.

Given the central role of retaining the Tridentine liturgy in the Traditionalist cause, it is obvious that the availability of cooperative priests is critical to the vitality and growth of the Movement. The shortage of such priests, and the generally unsuccessful efforts to recruit other priests into their ranks, has hindered the spread of the movement. The ORCM opened a seminary near its Monroe, Connecticut headquarters in 1973, but the venture proved unsuccessful and was discontinued after several months. In contrast to the American based Traditionalist organizations, the Society of St. Pius X is a priestly association with a bishop at its head who has the power to ordain priests. In practical terms, this means that the Society has a means of producing a resource critical to the survival of the Traditionalist Movement. Despite papal censorship and official suspension, Archbishop Lefebvre cannot be deprived of his power to ordain valid priests, although these priests are celebrating a Mass that is now considered illicit by the Vatican. I have often heard the Society portrayed (by its own priests and lay supporters) as the only Traditionalist organization with "realistic potential" for the restoration of the faith, since only the Society can insure a continuous source of Traditionalist priests. By 1982, Archbishop Lefebvre will be ordaining nearly forty new priests annually. This prospect is strengthened by the Society's American seminary, located in Ridgefield, Connecticut, where plans are currently under way for a 1.2 million dollar expansion of the facilities.[25]

Any social movement needs members as well as leaders, laity as well as clergy. The majority of lay Catholics in the Traditionalist Movement are older adults socialized into preconciliar Catholic values who describe their religious upbringing as "good," "pious," "active." They are married and with families. Nearly half of them had held office in church organizations, while forty percent indicated that they attend Mass on a daily basis. These two factors of organizational and sacramental participation reflect a high commitment to the patterns of preconciliar Catholicism and may be especially relevant in assessing the appeal of the Traditionalist Movement for them.

There is no empirical support in either my interviews or in my questionnaire respondents for the hypothesis that the participation of these Traditionalist lay people is a vicarious compensation for disprivilege or economic insecurity. The majority are concentrated in the middle and upper-middle class as measured by income, occupation and education. A minority are Democrats; thirty-nine percent identify themselves as Republicans, and thirty-five percent as political Independents. Whether or not Traditionalist lay Catholics are otherwise "relatively" deprived is a matter of conjecture. There is a strong doctrine of double "election" in Traditionalist ideology: Catholicism as the one true faith founded by Jesus Christ; and Traditionalist Catholicism as the one true "remnant" faith. This elect status may appeal to individuals who seek firm assurance of salvation, both as Catholics in possession of the true faith, and as Catholics "holding fast" at a time of widespread apostasy.

One predisposing factor of some significance relative to participation in the Traditionalist Movement concerns whether or not the individual is a convert to Catholicism. As my contacts with Traditionalist Catholics expanded during the course of my research, I was struck by the large number of converts active in the movement. The reason why converts are attracted to Catholic Traditionalism may lie in the appeal of one of the central ideological motifs in the movement. Traditionalism arose, in part, as a response to the conviction among some Catholics that their church, under the pretense of renewal and updating, was being turned into a "Protestantized" version of Christianity. Criticism of ecumenism and of the "Protestant character" of the postconciliar church is a persistently derogatory theme in Traditionalist literature and public statements. Their apologists have been vociferous in berating the "false ecumenism" that causes a blurring of Catholic identity and leads to concessions to the "heretics." At the heart of the Traditionalist attack on the *Novus Ordo* is the contention that it is a "Protestant rite."

Converts to Catholicism, especially those whose earlier religious socialization occurred in one of the Protestant churches, are receptive to the notion that postconciliar Catholicism is beginning to resemble Protestant denominationalism. They are resentful because this is, after all, the tradition they deliberately left behind them. The following comments, variations of which I have heard repeated many times, convey a sense of the psychology of betrayal expressed by these individuals:

> As a convert to the Church since 1950, the confusion and dismay that have come over me since Vatican II are very great. I found myself being returned, against my will, to the very things I had left to become a Catholic. I sacrificed friendships by giving up Protestantism and embracing Catholicism. But now in the Catholic Church I am again confronted by the very Protestantism I once renounced, and I will not have any part of it.

Sociocultural Trends

It has been fashionable among some social scientists to seek extrapersonal explanatory factors for the initiation and development of religious movements. It must be observed, however, that such environmental influences are never acceptable as either sufficient or necessary causes for the existence of reform movements, whether progressive or traditional. Nevertheless, we do live and act in a structured sociocultural system where "social forces," external to the individual, are at work. I would like to emphasize, in conclusion, three alternative dynamics that merit serious consideration in our attempt to comprehend the strength and appeal of Catholic Traditionalism.

The first of these is the fact that religious movements, either progressive or traditional, are usually associated with periods of structural strain which involves a threat to sacred values and religious symbolism. The Second Vatican Council altered many aspects of Catholic thought and behavior. Some even saw it as a direct challenge to the essentials of the faith. People who held fast to cherished ideas that they believed to be both immutable and sacred were disturbed by the so-called "Spirit of Vatican II" which seemed to promote a radical disjunction with what had previously been construed as unalterable truths. Traditional Catholics include many people who seem psychologically incapable of adjusting to these changes, because to do so would mean to make an unacceptable compromise that contradicts the very basis of their religious identity.

Secondly, it has been a frequent complaint among Traditional Catholics that they were given no official opportunities to air their grievances, especially in the all-important matter of liturgical renewal. No one listened to them. In Smelser's language, the avenues to normative change were closed and there was no alternative except to cling to the fellowship of a value-oriented movement. Once the *Novus Ordo* Mass became the mandatory rite in the church, in 1971, the hierarchy was committed to its implementation. Catholic Traditionalists could not get the decision reversed, nor could they easily abandon the church, as many liberals (for other reasons) apparently did. The logic of the Traditionalist commitment to Catholic orthodoxy necessitated an institutional affiliation with a valid source of sacramental compensators. To remain attached to the Tridentine Mass after 1971 inevitably meant challenging the teaching authority of the church. Traditionalists were especially sensitive to the irony that while the hierarchy willingly tolerated widespread liturgical variations to meet the needs of diverse interest groups within the church, it refused to permit continued use of its own Tridentine rite, all the while proclaiming that there is no fundamental difference between the old and the new Mass.

Finally, the Traditionalist Movement in the Catholic Church is a sociological product of certain ideological segments that have been part of the historical Catholic mosaic since the Council of Trent. It is not that these ideas ''caused'' the Traditionalist Movement, but rather that they enhanced its ideological credibility in a self-fulfilling manner. One pertinent example is the Traditionalists' interpretation of current tensions in the church as the diabolical unfolding of a vast and sinister plot of various ''enemies'' who are trying to infiltrate and subvert the church from within.

The notion that there is a dangerous ''fifth column'' at work inside the church may seem paranoid to less concerned observers, but it draws historic reinforcement from a long line of papal warnings and admonitions that such machinations were entirely possible. There has to be constant vigilance against such dangers, as exemplified in Pope Pius X's encyclical, *Pascendi Gregis*, warning against the ''threat'' of modernism. Furthermore, at the level of popular Catholic folk piety, these fears seem to be legitimated by apparitions like Fatima, allegedly warning of a period of widespread apostasy even in the highest echelons of the church.

Catholic Traditionalists have woven these motifs into a coherent world view that explains the contemporary malaise in the church and shapes their response to it. These ideological factors are deeply embedded in the historical character of Catholicism itself and they play a particularly poignant role in explaining the appeal of this Catholic religious alternative.

NOTES

1 Rodney Stark and William Sims Bainbridge, ''Of Churches, Sects, and Cults: Preliminary Concepts for a Theory of Religious Movements,'' *Journal for the Scientific Study of Religion*, 18, no. 2 (June 1979): 117-32.

2 See Ralph Turner and Lewis Killian, *Collective Behavior* (Englewood Cliffs, N.J.: Prentice-Hall, 1972). This is denied by Ross Roberts and Robert Kloss, "Religion as an Alternative," *Social Movements* (St. Louis: Mosby, 1979), pp. 60-64.

3 See Theodore M. Steeman, "The Underground Church: The Forms and Dynamics of Change in Contemporary Catholicism," in Donald R. Cutler, ed., *The Religious Situation: 1969* (Boston: Beacon Press, 1969), pp. 713-48.

4 *The Order of the Mass: General Instruction* (Washington, D.C.: U.S. Catholic Conference, 1969), p. 2. The so-called "Tridentine Rite" traces to the Twenty-Second Session, in H.J. Schroeder, *Canons and Decrees of the Council of Trent* (St. Louis: Herder, 1960), pp. 144-59.

5 Remarks made by Pope Paul VI on May 24, 1976 to the Consistory of Cardinals. Quoted in Michael Davies, *Apologia Pro Marcel Lefebvre* (Dickinson: Angelus Press, 1979), p. 176.

6 Steeman, p. 718.

7 See John Krote, *View From the Border: A Social Psychological Study of Current Catholicism* (Chicago: Aldine, 1971).

8 Representative conservative critics of liberal-inspired *aggiornamento* are Dietrich von Hildebrand, *Trojan Horse in the City of God* (Chicago: Franciscan Herald Press, 1967); George Kelley, *The Battle for the American Church* (New York, Doubleday, 1979); James Hitchcock, *Catholicism and Modernity: Confrontation or Capitulation?* (New York: Seabury, 1979).

9 For a Traditionalist critique see Michael Davies, *Liturgical Revolution III: Pope Paul's New Mass* (Dickinson: Angelus Press, 1980); from the conservative perspective see James Hitchcock, *The Recovery of the Sacred* (New York: Seabury, 1974).

10 Neil J. Smelser, *Theory of Collective Behavior* (New York: Free Press, 1963), pp. 313-82.

11 For example, see James F. Wathen, *The Great Sacrilege* (Rockford, Ill.: TAN Publishing Co., 1971).

12 This theme is found in such authors as Maurice Pinary, *The Plot Against the Church* (Los Angeles: St. Anthony Press, 1967); Clarence Kelly, *Conspiracy Against God and Man* (Belmont, Mass.: Western Island Press, 1974); and Rudolph Graber, *Athanasius and the Church of Our Time* (Buchs: Gerard Cross, 1974).

13 Smelser, pp. 270-313.

14 See the full text of "Constitution on the Sacred Liturgy," in Walter M. Abbott, ed., *The Documents of Vatican II* (New York: America Press, 1966), pp. 137-78.

15 See James Likoudis and Kenneth Whitehead, *The Pope, the Council*

and the Mass (Hanover, Mass.: Christopher Publishing House, 1981). The authors are officers in Catholics United for the Faith, an association of Conservative Catholics founded in 1968, and the largest of its kind.

16 For a Traditionalist account of the Archbishop's difficulties with Rome, and favorable to him, see Michael Davies, *Apologia Pro Marcel Lefebvre.*

17 Radko K. Jansky, *World-Wide Catholic Traditionalist Directory* (1981). Professor Jansky has published and circulated this directory since 1970.

18 They saw a contradiction between the *Syllabus of Errors* (1864) and *Dignitatis Humanae Personae* (1965), the Council's Declaration on Religious Freedom.

19 Ralph M. Wiltgen, *The Rhine Flows Into the Tiber* (Devon: Augustine Publishing Co., 1978); see also Dietrich von Hildebrand, *The Devastated Vineyard* (Chicago: Franciscan Herald Press, 1973).

20 See Hitchcock, *Catholicism,* p. 101.

21 Contrast, for example, Hitchcock's *The Recovery of the Sacred,* with Wathen's *The Great Sacrilege.*

22 Patrick Henry Olmor, *Questioning the Validity of the Mass Using the All-English Mass* (Reno: Athanasius Press, 1969). Meanwhile, Catholic feminists insist that the term "for all men" be changed to "for all persons."

23 These issues are treated by Gerald J. Dewey, "Role-Conflict: The Priest in a Postconciliar Church," in William T. Liu and Nathaniel J. Pallone, *Catholics/U.S.A.: Perspectives on Social Change* (New York: Wiley & Sons, 1970), pp. 75-110.

24 Archbishop Lefebvre, "The Ordination Sermon," pamphlet (Dickinson: Angelus Press, 1976).

25 "An Appeal from Archbishop Lefebvre," brochure distributed September 18, 1980.

The Electronic Churches

Jeffrey K. Hadden

In recent years the electronic church has become a source of great controversy. The initial critics, largely mainline Protestant leaders, charged that the electronic church constitutes a threat to local congregations.[1] The television preachers, critics argued, make it too easy for people to get their religion in the comfort of their living rooms. The perceived threat of losing communicants from the pews and dollars from the offering plate has resulted in a barrage of wide-ranging attacks on the televangelists.

In 1979 a few of the syndicated televangelists began airing partisan political views on a wide range of issues. Jerry Falwell, for example, founded a political organization he called The Moral Majority, and James Robison accepted the vice-presidency of another religious-political organization, The Roundtable. This move of a handful of televangelists into the political arena resulted in additional volleys of criticism being hurled at the electronic churches.[2] Mainline Protestants, who had earlier perceived religious telecasting as a threat, were joined by large sectors of the Catholic and Jewish communities as well as by liberals in the secular society who feared the mixing of evangelical zeal and right-wing politics.

Neither of these controversies is likely to dissipate in the near future. During the current decade, it appears quite likely that we will witness yet a third dimension of the electronic church controversy—the utilization of the airwaves to develop both new denominations and possibly new religions.

The seeds of both new denominations and new religious movements are already apparent in existing religious programming. Why this is so can be more easily grasped if one understands (1) *how* the electronic church developed, (2) *who* largely controls it and why, and (3) *why* it has been

159

so phenomenally successful during the past decade. The first objective of this chapter will be to establish these linkages. Having accomplished this task, the paper will then analyze why and how new denominations and new religions will be likely to emerge.

To anticipate the first task to be accomplished, let us note that there exists an almost inexorable relationship between the way in which the electronic church developed and the people who control it, which ties in with the reasons why they have been successful. First, the electronic church was made possible by rapidly expanding technologies that have revolutionized communication possibilities. At the center of this communications revolution is the computer, the utilization of which is obviously not denied to other religious organizations.

The electronic church is utilized and controlled predominantly by evangelical Christians because the logic and imperatives of the technology are compatible with their theological stance toward proselytization. The more reserved orientation toward proselytization on the part of the mainline Protestant churches, as well as their somewhat more complex theology, places serious restrictions on their ability to engage in the "market model"[3] implicit in the electronic church.

Finally, the phenomenal success of the electronic church during this past decade is, in part, a function of the intelligent application of the available technology. But more importantly is the drift—some would say stampede—of American culture towards conservatism. Dean Kelley's perspective analysis of why conservative churches are growing is correct in the identification of "certainty," "ultimate answers" and "meaning" as central to the evangelical success formula.[4] These components are central also to the success formula developed by the televangelists.

Stages of Growth

The growth and expansion of the electronic church parallel the development of all modern electronic communication. Historically, there have been three crucial communications revolutions: the invention of writing, the invention of movable type, and the advent of electronic communication, which is barely 100 years old, dating from the invention of the telephone. The development of the electronic church has been affected by three distinct generational phases of electronic communications. The first begins with the birth of the radio. The first voice was transmitted by radio in 1906,[5] and Congress acted in 1912 to establish licensing procedures. The inauguration of programmed professional radio broadcasting dates only to 1920 in Pittsburgh—and the church was there almost from the beginning. Within a month of regular broadcasting, radio station KDKA in Pittsburgh carried a live broadcast from Calvary Episcopal Church. Radio exploded in America in the 1920s. Within five years there were over six hundred stations. Fully ten percent of these stations were owned by religious organizations, and most engaged in some religious broadcasting.[6]

The second generation of electronic communication emerged with television during the 1950s. By the end of that decade nine of every ten households possessed at least one TV set. The technology and cost of television initially required a much greater centralization of broadcasting than was the case with radio. This meant a much narrower selection of programming. Nevertheless, religious telecasting was available almost from the beginning of this marvelous medium. Its first star was Fulton Sheen, the Catholic bishop with a twinkle in his eye, an impeccable delivery— and an angel to clean his chalkboard.[7]

But evangelicals, who eventually would dominate television airwaves, early recognized the potential of this medium.[8] In 1952 when Rex Humbard spotted a crowd gathered at the window of a department store in Akron to watch this marvelous new gadget called a television set, he knew immediately he had to put it to work broadcasting the gospel. He left his family of itinerant tent preachers and settled down in Akron so that he could start a television program. Oral Roberts brought the cameras into his gospel tent in the mid-50s. At about the same time, a young man named Jerry Falwell founded a Baptist church in an abandoned soft drink bottling plant in Lynchburg, Virginia. Long before he had any dreams of developing a nationwide ministry, he used television to build a 17,000 member congregation.

The third phase of electronic communications is not so easily dated. In some respects it can be considered an integral part of electronic ministries from the outset.[9] In another sense, the sophistication of the communication techniques, based on computer technology which permits rapid storage and retrieval of information, is so vastly improved as to represent a qualitative rather than a quantitative advance. Also critical to this third generation of electronic communication is the creation of feedback loops which permit direct communication between those who utilize the air-waves and their audiences.

From fairly early in radio broadcasting, many religious programs were financially dependent for survival on listening audiences. The most common and probably most successful technique to encourage listener support was to offer free printed materials (at times these were available for sale or for a ''love offering''), and to compile a mailing list of names of those who responded. For the most part, early electronic preachers knew little about the audiences they were dependent upon for contributions. This remained essentially true well into the 1960s.

The first revolutionary breakthrough in communicating with audiences was pioneered by Pat Robertson on WYAH-TV in Portsmouth, Virginia. Telephone lines installed to receive pledges during a 1963 telethon to keep the tiny station on the air were transformed into prayer lines. In

1980, Robertson's Christian Broadcasting Network handled 1.9 million calls requesting prayer and counseling.Twenty-four hour prayer and counseling lines have become an integral part of many of the electronic churches.

In its development, the electronic church is first of all a manifestation of a rapidly expanding technology which has revolutionized all communication. At the core of the revolution is the computer, with its continually accelerating speed of operation and a sharply declining per-unit cost. Without the computer, the modern telephone centers operated by Robertson, Jim Bakker and others would not be possible. And without the parapersonal services performed by volunteer counselors, it is doubtful that these electronic church enterprises could long operate in the black. Persons who call for prayer or counseling make up an important part of the mailing lists the electronic churches use to solicit money.[10]

Again computer technology is at the heart of fundraising. The mailing lists of contributors and potential contributors of the major electronic church operations number quite literally in the millions. The practical value of the computer is that it allows the preachers to mount giant direct-mail campaigns, sending out millions of fundraising letters as if passing one huge collection plate. By concentrating on the names and addresses of those who pay off, they can work on upgrading the size of contributions while simultaneously reducing the overall costs of fundraising.

This technology is applied widely in voluntary associations, business, government and politics. Unlike the original undifferentiated mailing lists, the new systems are such that a substantial amount of information about the people behind the names and addresses can now be compiled. This information can be stored, sorted and retrieved with lightning speed at nominal cost. In the specialized trade of direct mail, promoters constantly test different sales "pitches," different words and themes, to sell anything from coins and lingerie to politicians and magazines. The professionals gather once a year to distribute Golden Mailbox awards to the most successful marketeers. They can compare one sales pitch with another down to a thousandth of a percentage point of response.

The televangelists have yet to recognize the precision of such testing. To date they have largely adapted direct-mail technology to their own needs. Given a little more time and experience it is inevitable that they will become much more sophisticated. This greater sophistication will permit them *both* to better meet the needs of those in their audiences who write or call for help and to target fundraising appeals that meet their greatest vulnerabilities. Promoters of the electronic church encourage their listeners and viewers to write or call and share their problems and needs. Out of these pleas for help, the televangelists are building monumental data banks on the most intimate personal problems mentioned by the millions who phone or write.

Promoters and Proselytizers

Even the most casual observer will note that the religious airwaves are dominated by evangelicals, and that this is not accidental. Both the market economy and this technology are compatible with evangelical Christians' theological stance toward proselytizing. For better or worse, air time in our society is seldom available free of charge, and generally, the larger the audience one wishes to reach, the more it costs. Because utilization of the airwaves means participation in the free enterprise market, those who do so are overwhelmingly the ones who have something to sell.[11]

Evangelicals fit this criterion rather well, for they take literally Christ's command to "Go ye into all the world, and preach the gospel to every creature" (Mark 16:15). The airwaves have opened up, as never before, the possibility of spreading the Good News from sea to sea and around the globe. The basic question is: How are they to pay? And the answer is not difficult to find. While spreading the gospel, they encourage those who are already saved, or who have benefited from this electronic ministry, to contribute to the continuation of the good work.

Their success in raising money over the air is nothing short of phenomenal. At least a half-dozen of the major television ministries have operating budgets exceeding $50 million annually. A little simple arithmetic puts these large sums of money in perspective. All of the televangelists attempt to enroll viewers as regular contributors. By pledging a modest figure, usually $15 per month, you can become a "faith partner," "prayer key family member," "700 Club member," or whatever. A person who faithfully meets this pledge contributes $180 annually. But chances are that those who do this will also respond at least once during the year to one of the many special appeals made both on the air and via direct mail. Let us say they contribute, on average, an additional $20 for a total annual contribution of $200. At that rate, it takes only five thousand regulars to send in a million dollars. A quarter-of-a-million regulars, thus, could produce the $50 million budget. A fact sheet released by CBN in 1981 claimed 285,000 members of The 700 Club who donate $15 per month or more plus an additional 175,000 persons who have donated.

To enlist this many people, one has to reach a fairly large proportion of regular viewers. The evangelicals know how to do this. They go directly to the heartstrings. Get right with God. Get right with your loved ones. Get right with yourself. However the appeal is made, it is almost always emotionally charged. Obviously, it works. The evidence, however, suggests that many of their contributors do not stay with them long. Those who do can be counted on, with a little prodding, to increase their annual contributions.

What we see is a confluence of theological orientation toward proselytization and an organization of broadcast media which works to the benefit of evangelicals but against other religious groups. Communications specialists from Protestant and Catholic churches were warned by psychologist Liebert that the conflict over the electronic church "has every hallmark of an intensifying war of survival among battling Christian groups."[12] Evangelicals, because they believe they are being faithful to the great commandment to preach the gospel to all the world, have no difficulty using gimmicks and strong emotional appeals to raise the money to keep their programs on the air.

This is not the case with the mainline Protestant and Catholic traditions. First of all, they have a rather more sedate concept of evangelism, witness and Christ's commandment to spread the Good News. Furthermore, their tastes in worship do not appeal to the masses who think that Bach is a beer and Haydn used to be the quarterback of the Rams. Finally, the very thought of using the techniques required to raise money over the airwaves is simply repugnant to elites in the mainline traditions.

As a result, disgruntled mainliners remain on the sidelines complaining about the cheap grace and the dangerous political messages of the televangelists. In the meantime, the number of evangelicals who are getting in on the action is growing phenomenally. In 1980, the number of syndicated religious programs grew from sixty-six to ninety-seven. Whether the televangelists will be able to sustain their marvelous gospel spreading machines in the face of this much competition remains to be seen. The free enterprise system, which they all support, could be the very source of their financial collapse as they outbid one another for the most lucrative air times.

The million-dollar-a-week habit of the televangelists plus the increasing competition is likely to get some of them into financial trouble. While a few may go under, the electronic church will survive. The reason why this is so can best be understood by coming to grips with the persistence and significance of evangelical faith in American culture. When T. George Harris wrote "Our intellectuals are out to lunch...as unaware of religion's danger as its hope,"[13] he must certainly have been thinking also of pious liberals, religious and secular, who continue to treat evangelical religion as though it were an archaic religious form, peculiarly persistent in some regions of the country, but not a significant factor in American culture.

George Gallup declared 1976 "the year of the evangelical," but what that date really symbolized was the non-evangelicals' discovery that this sector of American society, previously presumed to be an insignificant fringe, was in fact very large. Perhaps it was also a turning point for evangelicals when they found that their world view was shared by a far larger proportion of American society than they had previously imagined.

It was the presence of this very large evangelical population which made the rapid expansion of the electronic church possible in the first place. To see the potential of the electronic church, we need to grasp the social context in which it grew and flourished. However unpopular the concept, resulting from its use by an unpopular president, "malaise" is an appropriate term to capture the American experience dating roughly from the assassination of John F. Kennedy. We have lost our leaders. We lost a war which tore us apart at home. We lost confidence in business and government. A president once admired by millions left office in disgrace. Inflation soars. Energy is scarce. International tensions mount one upon another. And for many who were over thirty during the sixties, the radical changes in young people's values and lifestyles underscored the loss of a taken-for-granted morality that was once as integral to American culture as baseball, popcorn and Chevrolet.

All of this bad news is so much the harder to take because television brings all the blood and guts and gore and hate and civil strife into the private sanctuary of our homes. And in addition to broadcasting the news, television magnifies the bad news by creating crime series and producing dramas that seem to condone lifestyles and language which affront the old values. It should have come as no surprise to learn that religious broadcasting would appeal to a segment of society angered and frustrated by all that has happened to disrupt their simpler and more tranquil world. And if one had understood how parapersonal communications and direct-mail technology could be combined to raise big money, one could have foreseen the growth in the electronic church that took place in the 1970s. But what can we expect of the electric church in the future?[14]

The Drive to Success

The electronic churches appear to be driven by two axiomatic principles. The first is that the television ministries themselves prosper in direct proportion to the boldness of their ancillary building projects. Oral Roberts built a university and is now endeavoring to complete a mammoth health care complex which includes a medical school. Jerry Falwell has launched a college he hopes will eventually become a university with 50,000 students. Pat Robertson is building a broadcasting network and a university. Jim Bakker's Heritage U.S.A. is a "total living center." Robert Schuller's Crystal Cathedral is a stunning architectural achievement.

The second axiom governing the television ministries is that they are most successful financially when they are, or appear to be, on the brink of financial disaster. The more they can persuade their audiences that they really are about to go bankrupt, the more the money flows into their mail rooms.

Professional money raisers feel they have a pretty good handle on the psychological dynamics of giving. Crises and bricks-and-mortar projects provide the best opportunity to tap the philanthropic instinct. People deserve a helping hand in their hour of great need—especially those who are doing the Lord's work. If responding to crises is pure altruism, the bricks-and-mortar projects provide the opportunity to contribute to something that will endure beyond one's own mortal presence on this earth. Those who contributed to the Crystal Cathedral could feel they were buying a little piece of immortality. Jimmy Swaggart, the latest of the televangelists to launch a major building project, offered his followers the opportunity to claim a square foot of his World Ministry Center for $50 or, for $500, one could be listed in the "Living Stone Honor Book." Jim Bakker, who cries on camera to punctuate the seriousness of his recurring financial crises, recently encouraged his followers to claim an acre of Heritage U.S.A. for a gift of $1,000 and help pay off the overdue mortgage. If you came to Charlotte, you could present your check to Jim in front of the PTL Club television audience.

If crises, real or contrived, and buckling projects are successful means for raising money, both have inherent dangers. Crises, like drug habits, have the tendency of requiring larger and larger doses to get a fix. Furthermore, there may be a limit to the number of times a televangelist can plead crisis before his loyalist followers begin to question the credibility of the claim. The propensity of the televangelists to equate their dreams to God's will, and their childlike trust that the almighty will deliver the bucks to pay for their projects, no matter how ambitious, portends a disastrous conclusion someday. That there are now more televangelists themselves competing for money from a total audience that has not increased appreciably in a half-dozen years may serve to hasten the day when one or more of the major ministries collapses.[15]

It is this precarious quality of the electronic churches that will eventually lead some of them into the franchising business. None of the televangelists has strong ties to a denominational body. Oral Roberts joined the Methodist Church some years back, but he is not subject to the discipline of that church body. Robert Schuller is a member of the Reformed Church of America, a point he remembers when he wants to remind people that he is a mainline Protestant. Jim Bakker's following is substantially Assemblies of God folks, but Bakker's ministry has no denominational ties. And so it is with most of the others—there are essentially no organizational constraints to hold them to an existing denomination.

One of the strongest arguments pointing to the inevitability of television ministers starting their own denominations is the fact that they are substantially dealing with a revolving door audience. Very often people get involved in watching religious programs during some personal crisis. The crisis having passed, they gradually drift away from the religious program(s) that brought them comfort. And as their viewing drops off, so also are they likely to drop the television minister from their list of charitable contributions. Viewed from an organizational perspective, this represents membership loss—and obviously, financial loss.

Audiences Into Congregations

If only a small proportion of persons who give to a television ministry could be converted into members of a local church organized by the televangelists, a much more stable financial base could be built. Good programming, magazines, cassettes, prayer lines, etc., all serve to reinforce commitment to the television ministries, but none of these services can be as effective in sustaining organizational commitment as regular face-to-face contact. Organizing audiences into congregations, thus, would substantially reduce the high turnover rate of contributors. Controlled from the top down, local congregations could be developed with little or no drain on revenues flowing in to support the national television ministry. And, since the local churches effectively belong to the national organization, their central mission activity would be to support the television ministry and its ancillary projects.

Persons who write or call the national ministry would

form the initial pool for recruitment of members. A skillful blending of communications technology and face-to-face recruiting techniques developed by groups like the Mormons could result in rapid church development. The televangelists and their local organizers could expect to receive a good bit of criticism for "robbing" the pews of other churches, but member "snatching" has been going on for a long time among proselytizing evangelicals. Furthermore, it is likely that recruiting would be most successful among persons who were dissatisfied with their present church affiliation and, hence, had sharply reduced their level of participation.

It is precisely because the audiences of the televangelists are constantly changing that television presents tremendous possibilities for building local congregations. In addition to the millions of churchgoing evangelicals who view religious television programs, there are literally tens of millions of unaffiliated but nominally believing Christians— the unchurched as shown by the 1978 Gallup study.[16] The potential pool of recruits, thus, is vast.

Research evidence indicates that door-to-door proselytizing is not a very effective way to recruit new members. But the disciples of televangelists could use this face-to-face contact to leave literature both about the local congregation and the television ministry. This kind of contact could produce multiple opportunities for follow-ups which do not exist when people say "no" to a doorknocker's invitation to enter their home for the purpose of proselytizing. The person contacted may decide to watch the television program —this is certainly much less threatening than allowing strangers into one's home. And having taken this step, one may then call or write or request prayer or materials offered on the program. And, eventually, the person who was turned away at the door may be invited back.

In short, the television ministries are faced with the serious need to develop a solid base of ongoing support. Founding the local congregations from the ranks of their television audiences provides an important channel for the accomplishment of this objective. The relative ease and limited cost of developing local churches, plus the potential rewards, will prove too tempting to pass up.

Some of the television ministries are better positioned than others to go into the franchising business. Perhaps best positioned to move in this direction is Jerry Falwell.[17] For all intents and purposes he already has the organizational structure in place. In addition to Liberty Baptist College, Falwell also founded and operates Liberty Baptist Seminary. It currently enrolls 170 students and Falwell claims that his seminary graduates have already started 200 new independent Baptist churches. Among his many ambitious goals for the current decade is the establishment of 5,000 new churches. Falwell denies any interest in founding a new denomination. To date, the new churches have no formal ties although some have taken the name Liberty Baptist. Falwell has great personal charisma and his students are intensely loyal to him. Were Falwell inclined, it would take little effort to transform independent Baptists into Falwellian Baptists.

Pat Robertson has in place a different kind of structure that could be transformed into the local congregations. The Christian Broadcasting Network maintains prayer and counseling centers in eighty-three cities in America. Many of the 10,000 volunteer counselors could be transformed into cadres of local congregations. And, the fact that counselors are usually only minutes away from those who call for prayers or help greatly facilitates the opportunities for face-to-face contact.[18] And, in this context, where people have voluntarily sought help, the probability of transforming contacts into converts is considerable.

Twenty-nine of CBN's prayer and counseling centers are full-time, 24-hour-a-day operations. Excluding Virginia Beach, the headquarters which receives calls nationwide, the average number of calls per month in early 1981 was almost 2,000. These roughly 25,000 calls a year could go a long way toward building a local church. Robertson does not yet have a seminary as part of CBN University, but he is a very resourceful man. Staffing local congregations, should he decide to go that route, would not create a great problem. If other televangelists are not as ideally organized to create new denominations as Falwell and Robertson, they still possess considerable resources to build churches that would owe allegiance to them.

One has to ask the question, of course, why have not the electronic churches already put their considerable resources to work to build new denominations. There are at least two important reasons. First, the electronic ministries are still very young. They have been too busy getting where they are now to have had time to mobilize resources to create local congregations. Only now have they developed national audiences and an organizational base to launch such a bold undertaking.

A second kind of response is that there is a significant psychological barrier. On the one hand there is a moral hesitancy. Almost all of the televangelists have repeatedly claimed that they provide a support and supplementary ministry to the local congregation—not competition or an alternative. It requires some mental gymnastics to begin deliberately to establish local churches while simultaneously denying that one is in competition with other local churches. The other source of hesitancy is motivated sheerly by an economic consideration. If they went about the business of organizing local congregations, would they alienate loyal viewers and financial supporters who are active in local congregations?

My own judgment is that neither moral hesitancy nor fear of economic reprisals will constitute serious barriers to organizing local congregations once the televangelists see the advantages and build the foundation to launch new church projects. Their rationale, of course, will be that they are filling a need unmet by others. Their experience in referring new converts to local congregations, they will argue, was too often unsuccessful because the local church failed to adequately shepherd the newly won souls.

The New Electronic Religion

If the cathode tube provides a powerful medium for creating new denominations in America, what of its potential to spawn new religions? The line that separates new religions from sectarian splits can be ambiguous. Whenever the group in question is socially visible, resolution of ambiguity is a political process. The Unification Church sees itself as an extension of the Christian faith, its leader being the recipient of special revelation and, perhaps, a special mission. The National Council of Churches of Christ in the U.S., supporting the generally negative reactions of America to Reverend Moon and his followers, has denounced the Unification Church's claim to being Christian and its application for membership.[19] The teachings of Jim Jones, leader of the People's Temple, moved well beyond even a remote resemblance to the Christian faith long before the tragedy that took 900 lives in Guyana. Still, in spite of the negative publicity People's Temple received in the Bay Area, the status of the group as a congregation in good standing with the Disciples of Christ was not challenged.[20] By any criteria, the teachings of Sun Myung Moon are closer to the core of Christian theology than the teachings of Jim Jones. Yet, the former's claim to Christian heritage is denied while the theological teachings of the latter remain largely unexplored.

If by a new religion in America we mean a faith which is generally perceived by political consensus not to be spiritually kin to one of the Protestant, Catholic or Jewish traditions, the prospect for creating new religions via the use of telecasting is fairly remote. Without being perceived as Christian (or Jewish) it would be extremely difficult to attract a sufficiently large and sympathetic audience to raise the monies required to pay for air time. Furthermore, any visible group that is perceived to be a "new"religion could be expected to be harassed by media and various government watchdogs alike. Hence, television would seem an unlikely medium to *build* a following for a group perceived to be new.

On the other hand, it is quite conceivable that a television minister, perceived to be in the Christian tradition, could gradually evolve principles or teachings which, again by political consensus, move so far beyond the range of accepted that they are defined as "new." To illustrate, let's look at a real case and project hypothetical developments.

Robert Schuller calls his theology "possibility thinking." He acknowledges debt to Norman Vincent Peale who wrote and preached about the "power of positive thinking." Both men steadfastly claim that the principles they teach are firmly anchored in the Christian faith. Let us assume that somewhere down the line Schuller begins to preach that sin is negative thought and original sin is self-doubt. Furthermore, let us assume he goes a step further and argues that many of the teachings of the Old and New Testament are antiquated myths that need to be jettisoned in light of knowledge about man gained by scientific methods. Would Schuller have overstepped the boundaries of Christian theology to create a new religion? Certainly many would think so. We need not project the scenario to see how others would respond in order to make the point that television ministers, because they tend to be charismatic and have large followings, have the potential to reshape religious doctrine—perhaps even to the point of creating new religions.

The central argument developed in this paper is that the electronic churches have moved beyond a role that might be described as ancillary or supportive to the local congregations. While existing evidence does not support the widely held assumption that the televangelists are succeeding to the detriment of the local congregation, there is clearly a structural basis for competition for scarce financial resources. It is argued here that growing competition among the televangelists themselves will almost certainly lead some of them to seek a solid base of support by establishing local congregations. This development most certainly will result in protracted conflict both with local churches and denominations most directly competitive theologically. Finally, it is suggested that the electronic churches have the potential to create new religions by evolving theologies that move outside the boundaries of existing groups. The potential for new religious groups to use the television airwaves to proselytize, however, is quite limited.

NOTES

1 In an earlier age, when radio was the medium, the question was raised, "Should Churches be Shut Off the Air?" *The Christian Century,* May 12, 1927.

2 See the discussion in Jeffrey K. Hadden and Charles E. Swann, "Born-Again Politics," in *Prime Time Preachers: The Rising Power of Televangelism* (Reading: Addison-Wesley, 1981).

3 Aspects of religious competition and cooperation were earlier discussed by Peter Berger, "A Market Model for the Analysis of Ecumenicity," *Social Research,* 30, no. 1 (Spring 1963): 77-93.

4 Dean M. Kelley, *Why Conservative Churches Are Growing* (New York: Harper & Row, 1972).

5 It was an informal religious program sent from Massachusetts to the ships at sea on Christmas Eve. See A.F. Harlow, *Old Wires and New Waves* (New York: Appleton-Century, 1936).

6 The audience of the "Radio Priest" was estimated in the tens of millions. See Wallace Stegner, "The Radio Priest and His Flock," in Isabel Leighton, ed., *The Aspirin Age* (New York: Simon and Schuster, 1949); also Charles J. Tull, *Father Coughlin and the New Deal* (Syracuse: Syracuse University Press, 1965).

7 See D.P. Noonan, *The Passion of Fulton Sheen* (New York: Dodd, Mead, 1972).

8 The chief charismatic predecessors of contemporary televangelists are studied by David Harrell, *All Things Are Possible* (Bloomington: Indiana University Press, 1975).

9 Everett Parker, David Barry, and Dallas Smythe, *The Television-Radio Audience and Religion* (New York: Harper and Brothers, 1955).

10 See Hadden and Swann, "This Business of TV Religion."
11 See Virginia S. Owens, *The Total Image, or Selling Jesus in the Modern Age* (Grand Rapids: Eerdmans, 1980).
12 Quoted by Hadden and Swann, p. 7.
13 He calls them "spiritual innocents." T. George Harris, "Introduction" to Hadden and Swann, p. xiv.
14 The term "electric" is preferred by Ben Armstrong, *The Electric Church* (Nashville: Thomas Nelson, 1979).
15 Exaggeration of the size of audiences is corrected by recourse to Arbitron figures. See William Martin, "The Birth of a Media Myth," *Atlantic*, 247, no. 6 (June 1981): 7, 10, 11, 16.
16 George Gallup, *Profile of the Christian Marketplace 1980* (Newport Beach: American Research Corporation, 1980).
17 See Gerald Strober and Ruth Tomczak, *Jerry Falwell: Aflame for God* (Nashville: Thomas Nelson, 1979).
18 Such personal contact with counselors predates the electronic church. See David Altheide and John Johnson, "Counting Souls: A Study of Counseling at Evangelical Crusades," *Pacific Sociological Review*, 20, no. 3 (July 1977): 323-48.
19 See the "study document" of the Commission on Faith and Order, "Critique of the Theology of the Unification Church," in Irving Louis Horowitz, ed., *Science, Sin and Scholarship* (Cambridge: MIT Press, 1978), pp. 102-18.
20 See the "corrective" analysis by James T. Richardson, "People's Temple and Jonestown: A Corrective Comparison and Critique," *Journal for the Scientific Study of Religion*, 19, no. 3 (September 1980): 239-55.

Home Church: Alternative Parish

Joseph H. Fichter

The Holy Spirit Association for the Unification of World Christianity, now widely known as the Unification Church, has become the main target of so-called anti-cultists, who condemn it as a dangerous alternative to conventional Western Christian American churches. I have argued elsewhere that the Unificationists have grown beyond the boundaries of a cult and are now a fully organized church with a scripture and a hierarchy. They comprise the four basic elements that social scientists declare essential ingredients of a religion: a belief system, a code of moral behavior, a pattern of worship and prayer, and a social structure. From this perspective the prediction of Frederick Sontag has already come true when he saw "the movement inevitably evolving into another established church."[1]

Although the Unification Church is a relatively new organized religion, having been founded as recently as 1954 in Korea, it has become an alternative option for the growing number of young Americans who select it in preference to the church or denomination to which they had previously been affiliated. It was formally proclaimed an alternative to Christianity when it was denied membership in the National Council of Churches in Christ. Its "heretical" doctrines were declared faulty, erroneous, inadequate and "incompatible with Christian teaching and belief."[2] Under this protocol, the Holy Spirit Association for the Unification of World Christianity is said to differ significantly from the mainline American Protestant churches. It is my intention, however, neither to spell out these differences, nor to demonstrate the considerable similarities the church has with traditional Christianity.

In many ways the Holy Spirit Association for the Unification of World Christianity is structurally similar to other well-established and highly organized religious denominations. It has a chain of command and communication from the newest fledgling member to the top hierarch. It is divided into regions of the country, like the judicatories of other churches, and has urban centers with appointed leaders analogous to ecclesiastical dioceses with their appointed bishops. It is at the lowest level of the structure where the Moonies are building the "home church" in place of the conventional parish or congregation. The focus of this discussion is an examination of this basic social unit as a substitute for the typical "worshipping community" to which Christians generally have become accustomed. What do the Unificationists mean when they talk about their home church?

Congregational Types

People who profess a religious faith and who live up to the mandates of their faith tend to identify themselves as church members by affiliating with a local group of the same religious persuasion. From a theological perspective one may say that the central and identifying social function of the congregation is the collective worship of God. Through song and ceremony, and through the preaching of the sacred scripture, the attention of the faithful is directed to the deity. Christians come together on Sunday morning—perhaps after they have already heard their favorite televangelist—in order to give glory to God, to praise the Lord, to recite prayers of petition and thanksgiving. The traditional rituals of the Jewish temple or synagogue are centered on the Lord. The buildings themselves, and the internal arrangement of the furniture, tables and altars and pews, are at least symbolically pointed to God.

While it is commonly said that people do not need a church building in which to worship God, and that God "may be found" in the beauties of nature—in the mountains, at the seaside—there have always been *places* of worship. The shrines of antiquity, the temples of Eastern religions and the cathedrals of Western Christianity, attest to the historical tendency to settle on specific locations where groups of people can gather in common demonstration of their religious beliefs. The place itself may become sacred as a magnet of pilgrims so that it no longer serves the particular local population for whom it was originally established. Similarly, the so-called "chapel of ease" attracts communicants in the downtown business and shopping districts where few parishioners actually reside. The noon Mass on weekdays, novenas and other religious services, are provided for virtual transients.

These traditional parochial structures endured for centuries wherever Christians gathered in permanent residential areas, and they are still the predominant form of congregational organization.[3] Although their central function is to proclaim the religious relationship with God, there appear to be many instances in which a secondary function, that of "fellowship," takes precedence. The Protestant congregation is described by Gibson Winter as a center of attraction for people of similar social status among whom the preservation of an exclusive community is of some importance.[4] While typical urban Catholic parishes focused on spiritual and sacramental functions for all Catholics who lived in the parochial territory, regardless of their social status, they tended to neglect any deliberate attempt to develop solidarity, or a sense of parochial belongingness. They were seen as a kind of spiritual "service station" with a franchise from the bishop that required no effort to build community.

In the recent past, however, with the advent of "new" religions, the influence of charismatic and pentecostal programs, and the "quest" for community among young people, there have occurred certain modifications in the conventional church groups, both the exclusive Protestant fellowship and the loosely structured Catholic parish. Some impetus was given by the Fathers of the Second Vatican Council for the renewal of both liturgy and community.

"Efforts also must be made to encourage a sense of community within the parish, above all in the common celebration of the Sunday Mass."[5] The study of American communes and utopias shows that in many instances the solidarity of the members was strengthened by their deep commitment to religious values. In other words, the more successful communes, those that endured for the longest period of time, were generally held together by shared religious beliefs and practices.[6] This is most obvious in centuries of experience in religious orders like the Benedictines, Carmelites and Franciscans.

While the basic organizational scheme tends to be similar in the conventional Christian congregations, some variety is introduced according to the size and type of population and location: small rural churches differ from large urban and suburban congregations. The Protestant congregation differs from the Catholic parish in the degree of lay participation in decision-making and the sharing of religious functions, but in both instances the central figure is still the minister. Changes are occurring. The so-called "intentional" community and the "covenant" community are offered as a substitute for the traditional parish.[7] This is meant to strengthen solidaristic ties in small primary groups of the faithful and also to facilitate the fulfillment of religious obligations. The central concept is unity and solidarity, the building of community.

It should be pointed out that the purpose of the Unificationist home church is neither to provide a place of worship nor to build a local spiritual community. In keeping with their ultimate objective of unifying all religions as well as all people, the Moonies have no hesitancy in attending religious services in Christian churches, Jewish synagogues, Islamic mosques or other houses of worship. There is an interesting parallel among the early disciples when Jesus was no longer among them. The *Acts* of the Apostles frequently recount that they "went up to the temple to pray," even though they participated also in the unique Eucharistic meal, the central act of collective worship, in the privacy of their own homes. Scripture scholars have called to our attention the role of "house churches" among the early Christians.[8] A more recent parallel developed when Chinese Christians were persecuted in the Cultural Revolution of the 1960s and their regular places of worship closed.[9] To substitute for the local church, they gathered in smaller numbers in many thousand "house churches," which soon came under the vigilance of the Peking government.

The Moonie Laity

While the Unification Church does not have an ordained clergy, it seems inappropriate to say that the leaders and full-time members are simply lay people. The members of the church are typically described as dedicated young people who accost strangers in airports, bus stations and on street corners, soliciting funds for their worthy causes, or inviting prospective converts to share a meal or to attend a lecture at the center. These are the full-time disciples of Reverend Moon whose religious zeal sometimes frightens parents and makes the clergy nervous. They exhibit a spiritual enthusiasm so alien to worldly materialistic patterns of American culture that they are often looked upon with suspicion, not only by secularists but also by adherents to the mainline churches. Enough has been publicized about the kidnapping and deprogramming of these young people that it need not be repeated here.

In a sense, these are the trained professionals of the movement, analogous to young Mormons on missionary duty, or to Catholic religious Sisters and Brothers, who do not aspire to the ordained ministry. When they first join the church, the Moonies perform the dual tasks of fundraising and witnessing, but with enough experience they soon assume the direction of a small mobile fundraising team travelling about the country. They may be appointed as leader, or central figure, of one of the numerous centers located in the larger American cities. Many specialized tasks, typical of expanding organizations, have to be filled by members at the New York headquarters as well as in foreign countries. Some college graduates among them may be chosen to attend the Unification Theological Seminary at Barrytown, New York, and after two years of study are sent to pursue a doctoral degree at one of the better known universities.

None of these full-time members, whether beginners at fundraising and witnessing, leaders of groups or at centers, special functionaries, seminarians or graduate students, can be called "laity" as the term is commonly applied to the ordinary members of typical church parishes. Nevertheless, the process of witnessing and evangelizing demonstrates that the church is "committed to the ministry of spreading by word and deed, the gospel of the Divine Lord and Saviour, Jesus Christ." They want to bring salvation to every human being, and not only to the fully committed members and leaders. This process reaches out to people who have jobs and families and social ties which they intend to maintain even after conversion to the Unification Church. Perhaps these are the ordinary laity, or lay associates, or even "marginal parishioners."[10] Eileen Barker describes them as "people who accept, or at least feel a fairly strong sympathy for, the teachings presented in *Divine Principle* but who, for various reasons, do not commit themselves to living in a center or to working full time for the UC."[11]

Except for the fact that they share the same adherence to the tenets of the Unification Church, these lay associates differ widely from the full-time Moonies. Males outnumber females by about two to one among the fully dedicated members, but this sex ratio is reversed among the associates. There is also an age difference, with the majority (80%) of the laity being over thirty years of age, while the same proportion of full timers is under thirty. Perhaps mainly because of this age difference, the associates are less well-educated and with fewer years of college schooling, but are also more likely to be married.

The prospective convert who is a permanent spinster or bachelor promises to raise a doctrinal embarrassment for the church. The religious vocation of the full-fledged Moonie is a preparation for the blessed state of matrimony with a Unificationist spouse chosen by Reverend Moon. This basic principle is important because the normal channel of salvation is the family lineage which brings redemption through blessed parents from generation to successive generations. This raises the question for prospective membership of persons who do not wish to be married, or who do not find the individual they would like to marry. At a Unification seminar the remark was made that the church's "theological emphasis is completely geared towards the notion of a heterosexual, monogamous marriage. With this as the center, other kinds of relationships do not seem possible or viable. Single people seem to be regarded somewhat like Cinderellas amidst the chosen people's family."[12]

It appears that as the number of lay converts increase and as the home church develops, room is being made among the associates for the bachelor and the single woman. Where statistics have been gathered we learn that approximately half of these laity are married, while three out of ten (28%) are separated, divorced or widowed, the remainder being single. This means that half of the lay associates are not now in the blessed state of marriage to which the fully committed members aspire, or have already reached. This may be a partial reason why many give the impression that "they had been leading lonely and unsatisfied lives. One of their most frequent complaints was that the Unification Church did not use them enough. Their existence indicated that the Unification Church might appeal to a wider constituency than that from which the full-time Moonie was drawn, but that it succeeded in doing so only as long as it did not demand the kind of unquestioning devotion and sacrificial life-style that the young unmarried Moonie was prepared to give."[13]

Origins of Home Church

The suggestion that some Moonie affiliates want the church to make use of them, give them something to do, provides a clue to the basic purpose of the home church and the manner in which it operates. As an alternative to the conventional local parish, the primary Unificationist objective is not to establish a place of worship, or to develop a close-knit fellowship. Their stated purpose is to administer to the needs of the people, to offer voluntary and friendly assistance to all individuals and families of the neighborhood. The Unification home church is not a building to which parishioners come for prayer and fellowship. The home church goes to the people, all the residents in an area of about four city blocks, containing 360 household units, regardless of their church affiliation. It is a church of service, a religious movement for giving rather than for receiving. All the people living within the designated neighborhood (which may be a college dormitory, a highrise apartment, or an institution) are the recipients of the Moonie ministry, rather than formally pledged members who are expected to provide financial support for the church.

This strategy of altruistic service is the main characteristic that sets the Unificationist home church apart from other local congregations and parishes. Although the use of the term, home church, became popular only in the summer of 1978 when Reverend Moon took the Barrytown seminarians to do missionary work in England and Scotland, the practice of altruistic service to strangers goes back to the pioneer days of the movement in Korea. It is a central theme of the Moonie theology of salvation that "we atone for our sins through specific acts of penance." The restoration of all things to the loving Father requires the believer to fulfill the "condition of indemnity."[14] Dedicating oneself to the service of others for a definite period of time is a means of atoning for the sins of humanity and satisfying the divine will.

It is a matter of record that Reverend Moon sent out his earliest converts on a forty-day pioneering mission; one of the first female followers was sent from Pusan to Taegu to work out this form of indemnity. This is still a practice among the Moonies and it is appreciated as an excellent preparation for the establishment of a home church. The trial period is reminiscent of the forty days during which the Hebrews doubted that Canaan was to be the Promised Land. Because of their lack of faith they were forced to wander in the desert forty years before God allowed them to enter Canaan. The individual Moonie sometimes says that these forty days of trial are his opportunity to ''gain Canaan'' for God as well as to gain the specific kinds of experience that will help in the successful operation of his home church.

A dedicated young German Moonie, who now has a responsible administrative position in the Unification Church, described this forty-day experience. He left Frankfurt with only twenty deutsche marks in his pocket and with no luggage in order to minister to the people in a rural community. He told us:

> This was a condition that existed already in the Korean church since twenty years. We had a preparatory gathering for three days at the training center. None of us had tried anything like this before. We were not even sure we could survive, but early on Saturday morning we left by train for our respective home church areas. The first night I slept at the Red Cross, and the next two nights in a barn. On Sunday morning I went to Mass, and afterwards offered to work for the priest. He was very friendly, but said he didn't need any help. During the week I offered to help at two Senior Citizens' Homes, but they also needed no help. I went from house to house to several hundred families, and just kept going back; I felt I had to do this to win the trust of the people.
>
> Early each morning I went to the train station to talk with people before they'd go to work. Some I just approached

and asked them to think about God this day, and they would
say "I'll really consider that." Others didn't know what to
say; they just smiled or they ignored me. One lady gave me
fifty marks so I could find a place to sleep. That was enough
to get a cheap hotel for three nights. I was selling the church
magazine, *Neue Hoffnung*, but I really didn't need much
money. I rented a room in a private home, and for the whole
period of six weeks I lived on something like 350 to 400
marks.

Gradually I got to know more families, old people who
were lonely, busy mothers for whom I could do errands,
foreign workers from Turkey who felt strange among their
Christian neighbors. What I was doing was an example of the
forty-day pioneer mission that prepares you for the eventual
home church, which is a place where you live regularly. I
have been able to keep some contacts with these people
even though I've been mostly in other places doing other
kinds of work in the church. I still think of that as my own
home church. During the year since I had that six weeks'
experience, more of the other Unificationists who have families and outside jobs have established home churches in their
own neighborhoods. We have not made as much progress in
Germany as they did in Korea, and more recently in England,
and maybe in America.

A Korean home church leader told us that he continues
to get inspiration from Reverend Moon who teaches his
followers to live for others and to cherish family life. This
leader has a full-time job in private industry as a section
chief in a large local factory. With his wife and children he
says that he "feels an obligation" to be concerned for the
360 families in his immediate neighborhood. Because of
some local anti-Moonie prejudice, they did not at first tell
the people that they are members of the Unification Church.
But their friendliness and their "good deeds" were soon
appreciated by many who began to enquire why they were
doing these things. After two years of such service they
were able to count only eleven families who had joined the
church, but they insisted that the purpose of the home
church was being fulfilled: to bring love and kindness and

service to people in the name of God. They reported also that in the fall of 1981 there were 230 home churches in the city of Seoul alone, and that similar home churches had been set up all over the Republic of Korea.

In Korea itself the Unification Church has evolved more extensively than anywhere else in the world, but it is still a minority even among Korean Christians. Many Unificationists in the city of Seoul are not yet personally committed to the home church movement. As a matter of current practice they attend religious service on Sundays—and sometimes on Wednesday evenings—at any one of thirty Unification Church centers, each of which is under the direction of a "district leader." This means that in Korea, unlike other countries where the Moonies live in community centers, the members of the church tend to be conventional parishioners, who live at home with their families and for the most part have conventional jobs in the private sector of the economy.

From this point of view the home church movement is a relatively new program in Korea, as it is in other countries. We have no reliable statistics on the number of church members who attend the thirty district church centers in Seoul although we have been assured that the number of Moonie converts is steadily growing. Let us assume that in each of the 230 home church areas a good rapport has been reached with all 360 households, and that each of these families averages five persons. The total persons thus contacted through the home church movement still constitute a small minority among the many millions of inhabitants in the capital city. One can only speculate about the direction the home church movement will take in countries other than its Korean birthplace.

While the activities of the home church encourage spontaneity and creativity, the worldwide experiences have begun to become formalized. After the Barrytown seminarians returned from their forty-day experience in England and Scotland in the summer of 1978, the seminary introduced into its curriculum a field work course on the home church program. Each student takes this course for one semester and is assigned a location for ministry to 360 households in one of the nearby towns. The pattern has spread also to those in graduate studies at various universities who in their spare time take responsibility for a definite number of living units in residence halls or in the vicinity of the campus. American church members who have married and settled down, whether as full-time functionaries of the church or as employees in some non-church occupation, are gradually developing a permanent ministry to their immediate neighbors. The ultimate dream is a network of contiguous home churches spread over the whole nation.

Social Reform

The Unification Church has been called a "world-transforming" movement which extends its influence beyond the spiritual conversion and salvation of individuals.[15] The church's ideology is geared to a complete reformation of all sociocultural institutions: education, politics, economics, and even recreation. The collective concern for the whole world population begins with personal purification and the spirituality of marriage and family life. Enthusiastic members give witness to prospective recruits who are invited to dinners, meetings, and the series of lectures explaining *Divine Principle*. The approach of the home church to the whole neighborhood delays this proselytizing activity and replaces it with a mission of service.[16] The material, social and psychological needs of the neighbors are met before any mention is made of religion. The primary intention, therefore, of the home church is not to increase the number of Unificationists, but to manifest God's love to fellow human beings.

The ideological progression to total world reform leads from personal piety to family renewal to the home church ministry in the neighborhood. The anticipated evolution of the home church as the starting place for the total reform of society may be compared to the development of the *communidades de base*, the grassroots movement among South American Catholics, commonly referred to as the Basic Christian Community.[17] Three stages may be discerned in the evolution of these local communities: (1) the formation of religious sub-groups intent upon prayer, gospel-sharing and sacramental devotions; (2) the second step is the group performance of social tasks, mutual aid within the neighborhood, improving collective facilities; (3) this is to culminate in the raising of consciousness, or a civic awareness and a commitment to the reform of the larger society.

While the ultimate goal of societal transformation—to restore the world to God—may be quite similar in these two forms of grassroots religious organization, certain dissimilarities are evident. The first difference is that the Basic Christian Community exists only among the poor and oppressed members of the Catholic population, and is neither attractive to, nor intended for, the bourgeoisie of whatever religion. The Unificationist home church is intended ultimately to exist everywhere and to reach out to people of all religions (or none) and of all social classes. Their universality is limited, and their development is delayed, only by the finite numbers of Unificationists available for the task.

Another important difference is the reversal of the first two stages: prayer that leads to social service, as compared with social service that leads to prayer. The Basic Christian Community starts with members of the same religion who gather for religious worship, bible study and prayer. Out of this comes a recognition that they have a moral right to be liberated from oppression, illiteracy, endemic illnesses, and they are motivated then to the second stage of mutual aid. The Unificationist home church begins at the second stage by immediately offering to alleviate the needs of families and households. The dedicated Moonie arrives as an individual to render service to any and all persons and families among the 360 households in the immediate neighborhood.

If there then evolves a stage of increased religiosity and spirituality it must be seen as an indeliberate consequence of the Moonies' selfless altruism.

The third stage of development in both approaches is the achievement of a better society, but the emphasis within the Basic Christian Community is on a group commitment, while in the Unificationist home church the emphasis tends to be on individualistic commitment. The Moonie doctrine is quite clear that personal reform is an absolute condition for social reform. No change or improvement of the larger social structures and cultural institutions is thinkable unless the people have first been converted.[18] Only when hearts and minds and behavior have been turned to God can we expect significant social transformation. The doctrine of the *Communidades* provides a different view: the notion that social reform can occur even before the citizenry has attained sanctity. On the other hand, a pious population may well continue to live in the midst of unworkable structures and oppressive institutions.

The program of social reform at the grassroots level differs significantly according to the respective views on Marxism. The Unificationists are so adamantly opposed to atheistic, materialistic Communism that they repudiate the analytical methods proposed by the father of Communism. The very concept of class struggle is seen as a Satanic attack on the Capitalist system. The members of the Basic Christian Community in South America, however, are the poor and the underprivileged now gradually becoming aware of their status as the working class. This awareness allows them to "accept Marxism as a tool, as a method of scientific analysis of reality that enables us to analyze the mechanism by which a society evolves . . . Understood in this way, Marxism is already, to a large extent, part of our present culture; it has in particular been adopted by the social sciences."[19] Even this analytical tool is anathema to the Moonies. The home church they establish among the proletariat is not likely to encourage any radical expression of class consciousness.

Social Welfare

The Unificationists who told us about their experience in serving 360 households in a specific area spoke frequently of *my* home church, an indication that this ministry was assumed as a personal vocation. The establishment of each specific home church is not the result of a mandate "from above," from New York headquarters, or from the state director of the church. The prime responsibility rests with the individual, fully dedicated Moonie who has had wide experience encountering strangers in fundraising and witnessing. "You go from door to door and tell the people you're a church missionary with a program of service to the community. We volunteer to help in their home if they need yard work, or small repairs, or housecleaning, or transportation for the elderly to go to the doctor, or to the store. We have a pickup truck to haul trash for them and a lawnmower to cut their front lawn."

The pattern of volunteer service, widely practiced in American society, is almost always in affiliation with an organization like the Red Cross, the St. Vincent de Paul Society, a hospital auxiliary, the United Way, where the individual cooperates with fellow volunteers in an on-going group. The Moonie volunteers to make face-to-face contact with complete strangers. I asked a center leader how people receive them and their offer of help. "At first they are reluctant to take help from a stranger. You actually have to develop a friendly relationship before they even let you help. Either they are suspicious of strangers or they have a feeling of pride that they can take care of themselves and their own needs. Once in a while some people want to take advantage of the church member and want you to come three hours a day twice a week. I have to stress to the home church members that they might have to set a time limit to the service they can give to any one household."[20] When the home church members settle permanently in a fixed residential area—which is becoming increasingly frequent as married Moonies establish their own families—volunteer participation tends to become more organized. More associates are influenced by their good example: volunteers help to supervise playground activities, give instructions to retarded children, encourage teenagers to clean the streets and sidewalks of the neighborhood. In one home church area the members held a drive to collect newspapers and aluminum cans for recycling; in December they collected and donated canned goods to the local Food Bank for emergencies. Another home church organized a musical group that provided entertainment on various occasions in the neighborhood.

In some of the larger cities where the number of associate members have grown rapidly the Unification home churches cooperate ecumenically in the Council for Church and Social Action. Distribution of food becomes a regular program where the members gather fresh produce from the city markets and distribute it at cost. Programs for transportation of the elderly are conducted for the aging population; also programs for the protection of citizens against juvenile crime as well as for the rehabilitation of teenage delinquents. The largest cooperative effort in the country occurs through the International Relief Friendship Foundation which was established by the Unification Church as a relief service to third world countries.

The dedicated service of the individual Moonie to the residents in his home church area logically evolves into cooperative efforts with other persons and other groups. The individual alone cannot complete the close sinless relationship with God the Father because in the providence of God the person cannot be isolated from other human beings. The Christian notion of a community of saints places also an emphasis on the horizontal relationship of one person to another. The dedicated Moonie tells us that "salvation takes place within a community in a world of people who live together not simply as individuals connected to God but also related to one another."[21]

Reverend Moon has deliberately clarified the purpose of the home church as the service to humanity, and not as the conversion of non-Moonies to the church, or the development of fellowship, or the establishment of a place of worship. Nevertheless, it is quite logical to expect that these secondary aims will be achieved, and they will be ultimately attributable to the demonstration of love and service on the part of the Moonie for the non-Moonies. One may view this from the perspective of the missionary who is fulfilling a divine vocation of evangelization to the unsaved, but whose missionary zeal has been limited to the simple mundane task of service to strangers. The task does not stop there. The Moonie vision encompasses a God-centered home church linked with all other home churches that reflect the restoration of the Kingdom of Heaven on earth.

The Family Model

From a structural perspective we are free to conclude that the home church is an alternative to the conventional parish or congregation, but it is not an alternative to the blessed family. In one of our interviews, Reverend Moon was quoted as saying that "home church is our destiny. It is not a witnessing technique like reaching people on the street or inviting them to a meal or a lecture. The home church is much deeper than this because it is integral to the building of God's kingdom on earth. It is really the future direction of human destiny in the divine plan. If there had been no sin in the Garden of Eden, if Adam and Eve had not fallen, theirs would have been the first home church. They would have grown to perfection with God as partner of their marriage and family. As their children multiplied into a tribe and then into a nation every God-centered family would have been a home church."

Focusing on the home church as a unit of sociological analysis—as we have done in this paper—could lead to the erroneous conclusion that it may exist in isolation from the total Unification Church. It is essential to realize that in the Unificationist conceptual framework the religious collectivity itself is a family, and that the main channel for the restoration of sinful humanity to God is the family. The Moonies want to use the terms "family" and "church" interchangeably. They like their church to be known as the "Unified Family," in which Reverend Moon and his wife are the "True Parents" of the members who are spiritual children. The church is the family, and the family is the church, but the Unification movement has not yet evolved to the point where the home church can be seen as a family-type social unit.

At the present time in Europe and the United States, and to some extent also in Japan and Korea, the Moonies experience primary familial relationships only in the specific communities where the full-time members reside. Spiritual siblings, fully committed sisters and brothers, recognize each other as children in the God-centered Unification family. When the pastor of a Catholic territorial parish says that "we are a big happy family," he is speaking in hyperbole, suggesting that the loving primary relations of the ideal family are imitated by the parishioners. The Moonie in the typical urban center of the church wants the group to be much more than hyperbole because the basic theme of personal salvation is through the family. The ultimate goal of God's creation rests on the four position foundation, manifested as "God, husband and wife and their offspring."[22]

The typical Unification community where the members live, and out of which they carry on their full-time vocation, is not the basic model for the home church. It is in some ways similar to the urban center where Franciscan friars live in community and minister to the needs of the faithful, most of whom are strangers to them. The Moonie center also provides lectures, distributes literature and conducts religious services. Like the Franciscans the full-fledged Moonies share their lives, their tasks and their belongings, and address each other as members of the same family.

In looking at the structural development of the Unification Church, it seems important to note that Reverend Moon does not talk of plans to organize parishes, dioceses, judicatories, or vicariates. "I emphasize that our movement has always been centered upon families as the basic unit of heavenly society. The family emphasis is always the same. This means that more blessings in marriage will be given, more children will be born, more families will be created. Then we will become elevated from the present communal type of centers to family-oriented homes. The family will always be the basic unit of happiness and cornerstone of the kingdom of God on earth and thereafter in heaven."[23]

In the final analysis, the home church should probably be accepted as a manifestation of the divine program that Reverend Moon sees in evolution throughout all history, a restoration of humanity "with all the races standing side by side as brothers centered on Christ, who is the nucleus of Christianity. What makes Christianity different from other religions is that its purpose is to restore the one great world family which God had intended at the creation. This is to be accomplished by finding the True Parents of mankind through whom all men can become children of goodness through rebirth."[24] The sense of urgency with which Moonies serve non-members through the home church is built on the conviction that all will eventually be welcomed into God's "one great world family."

NOTES

1 Frederick Sontag, *Sun Myung Moon and the Unification Church* (Nashville: Abingdon, 1977), p. 201.

2 See the "Critique of the Theology of the Unification Church as Set Forth in *Divine Principle*," in Irving Louis Horowitz, ed., *Science, Sin, and Scholarship* (Cambridge: MIT Press, 1978), pp. 103-18.

3 Joseph H. Fichter, "Conceptualization of the Urban Church," *Social Forces*, 31, no. 1 (October 1952): 43-46.

4 Gibson Winter, *The Suburban Captivity of the Churches* (New York: Macmillan, 1962).

5 "Constitution on the Sacred Liturgy," of Vatican II, art. 42

6 These are called "alternatives to established society" by Rosabeth Moss Kanter, *Commitment and Community* (Cambridge: Harvard University Press, 1972), p. vii.

7 Marguerite Bouvard, *The Intentional Community* (Port Washington: Kennikat Press, 1975); also Margaret Poloma, "Christian Covenant Communities," in Charles De Santo, Calvin Redekop, and William Smith-Hinds, eds., *A Reader in Sociology: Christian Perspectives* (Scottsdale: Herald Press, 1980), pp. 609-30.

8 Discussed by F.V. Filson, "The Significance of the Early House Churches," *Journal of Biblical Literature*, 58 (1939): 105-12; see also Robert Banks, *Paul's Idea of Community: The Early House Churches in Their Historical Setting* (Grand Rapids: Eerdmans, 1980).

9 Reported in *Time*, October 19, 1981, p. 109. Destructive persecution of the Unification Church in Brazil has also been reported in the news media. See Kenneth Freed, "Moonies Met by Mobs, Hostile Officials in Tolerant Brazil," *Los Angeles Times*, Tuesday, September 8, 1981, pp. 6-7.

10 Joseph H. Fichter, "The Marginal Catholic: An Institutional Approach," in *Social Relations in the Urban Parish* (Chicago: University of Chicago Press, 1954), pp. 56-67.

11 Eileen Barker, "Who'd Be A Moonie?" in Bryan Wilson, ed., *The Social Impact of New Religious Movements* (Barrytown, N.Y.: Unification Theological Seminary, distr. Rose of Sharon Press, 1981), pp. 59-96.

12 Remark of Unitarian minister George Exoo, in Darrol Bryant, ed., *Proceedings of the Virgin Islands' Seminar on Unification Theology* (Barrytown, N.Y.: Unification Theological Seminary, distr. Rose of Sharon Press, Inc., 1980), p. 306.

13 Barker, p. 93.

14 The concept of "restoration through indemnity" is found in *Divine Principle*, pp. 222-27, and is discussed by Young Oon Kim, *Unification Theology* (New York: Holy Spirit Association for the Unification of World Christianity, 1980), pp.229-33.

15 This theme is discussed by Anson Shupe and David Bromley, "Characteristics of World-Transforming Movements," *Sociological Analysis*, 40, no. 4 (Winter 1979): 326-28.

16 The advice of Rev. Won Pil Kim: "Be a servant of servants to your

360 homes and love them wholeheartedly, not in a self-centered way. You might think that you can change people with your wisdom and knowledge, but the only way change will happen is through sacrificial love." *Today's World*, 2, no. 9 (September 1981): 29.

17 Gottfried Deelen, "The Church on its Way to the People: Basic Christian Communities in Brazil," *Cross Currents*, 30, no. 4 (Winter 1980-81): 385-419. Basic Communities were twice the theme of *Pro Mundi Vita Bulletin*, July 1976 and April 1980.

18 The primary condition for a better society is the multiplication of born-again Christians. "Fundamentalism as a Social Movement," in H. Paul Chalfant, Robert E. Beckley, and C. Eddie Palmer, *Religion in Contemporary Society* (Sherman Oaks: Alfred Publishing, 1981), pp. 227-58.

19 Deelen, p. 405, quoting Bishop Marcelo Cavalheira of João Pessoa.

20 Unificationists are welcomed by the elderly whose homes they clean in Northern New Jersey, but the favorable news report was head-lined: "Moonies Get Their Foot in the Door," *Bergen Record*, June 22, 1981.

21 Anthony Guerra, quoted in Darrol Bryant, ed., *Proceedings of the Virgin Islands' Seminar on Unification Theology*, p. 175.

22 *Divine Principle* 5th ed. (New York: Holy Spirit Association for the Unification of World Christianity, 1977), p. 32.

23 As told to Frederick Sontag, *Sun Myung Moon and the Unification Church* (Nashville: Abingdon, 1977), p. 157. More recently he said that "in the future, our organization will become completely home church. National leaders, center leaders—everyone—will do home church work. Thus, the era of mobile activity will draw to a close, and everyone will settle down." *Today's World*, 2, no. 9 (September 1981): 16.

24 *Divine Principle*, p.123.

PARTICIPANTS IN THE CHICAGO CONFERENCE ON "ALTERNATIVE RELIGIONS: RESEARCH AND STUDY"

Gordon Anderson graduate of Unification Theological Seminary; now a Ph.D. candidate at Claremont Graduate School, Claremont, California

William Sims Bainbridge Associate Professor of Sociology, Harvard University, Cambridge, Massachusetts

Eileen Barker Professor of Sociology, London School of Economics and Political Science, England

David G. Bromley Professor and Chairman, Dept. of Sociology, University of Hartford, West Hartford, Connecticut

William D. Dinges Assistant Professor, Dept. of Philosophy/Religion, Ithaca College, Ithaca, New York

Franz Feige graduate of Unification Theological Seminary; now a Ph.D. candidate at Drew University, Madison, New Jersey

Joseph H. Fichter Professor of Sociology, Loyola University of the South, New Orleans, Louisiana

Frank K. Flinn Consultant in forensic theology and Religion Editor, The Edwin Mellen Press, Toronto, New York

Jeffrey K. Hadden Professor of Sociology, University of Virginia, Charlottesville, Virginia

Virginia Hearn Editor and writer, Berkeley, California

David S.C. Kim President, Unification Theological Seminary, Barrytown, New York

Robert Lively Assistant Professor of Religion, University of Maine, Farmington, Maine

John T. Maniatis Head librarian, Unification Theological Seminary, and executive director of New ERA, Barrytown, New York

David Martin Professor of Sociology, London School of Economics and Political Science, England

J. Gordon Melton Director, Institute for the Study of American Religion, Evanston, Illinois

Mike Mickler graduate of Unification Theological Seminary; now a Ph.D. candidate at Graduate Theological Union, Berkeley, California

Robert L. Moore Associate Professor of Psychology and Religion, Chicago Theological Seminary, Chicago, Illinois

Larry G. Murphy Associate Professor of History of Christianity, Garrett-Evangelical Theological Seminary, Evanston, Illinois

Jerome A. O'leary Director emeritus, Institute of Pastoral Studies, Chicago, Illinois

Stephen Post graduate of Unification Theological Seminary; now a Ph.D. candidate at University of Chicago Divinity School, Chicago, Illinois

Mel Prosen Associate Chairman, Dept. of Psychiatry, Rush Memorial Hospital, Chicago, Illinois

Rodney J. Sawatsky Director of Academic Affairs, Conrad Grebel College, University of Waterloo, Ontario, Canada

Whitney Shiner graduate of Unification Theological Seminary; now a Ph.D. candidate at Yale University Divinity School, Hartford, Connecticut

Larry D. Shinn Professor of the History of Religion, Oberlin College, Oberlin, Ohio

Anson Shupe, Jr. Professor of Sociology, University of Texas, Arlington, Texas

Rodney Stark Professor of Sociology, University of Washington, Seattle, Washington

Melinda Bollar Wagner Assistant Professor of Anthropology, Radford University, Radford, Virginia

James S. Wolfe a Ph.D. candidate at Iowa State University, Ames, Iowa

Richard Woods, O.P. Institute of Pastoral Studies, Loyola University, Chicago, Illinois

Other Books on the Unification Movement

Distributed by
The Rose of Sharon Press, Inc.
G.P.O. Box 2432
New York, N.Y. 10116

$10.95

ISBN 0-932894-14-3

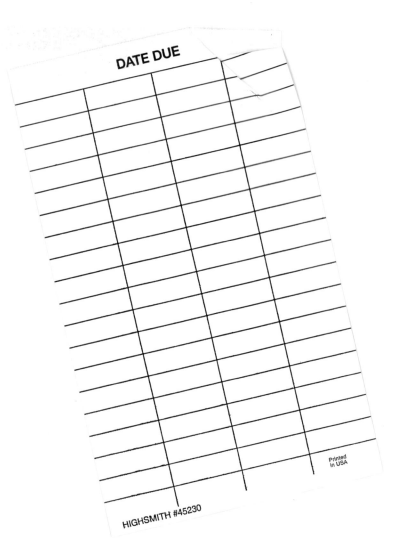

DATE DUE

Printed
in USA

HIGHSMITH #45230